ROUTLEDGE LIBRARY EDITIONS:
BUSINESS AND ECONOMICS IN ASIA

Volume 29

REPORT ON TRADE CONDITIONS IN CHINA

REPORT ON TRADE CONDITIONS IN CHINA

HARRY R. BURRILL AND RAYMOND F. CRIST

Routledge
Taylor & Francis Group

LONDON AND NEW YORK

First published in 1980 by Garland Publishing, Inc.

This edition first published in 2019
by Routledge
2 Park Square, Milton Park, Abingdon, Oxon OX14 4RN

and by Routledge
52 Vanderbilt Avenue, New York, NY 10017

Routledge is an imprint of the Taylor & Francis Group, an informa business

British Library Cataloguing in Publication Data
A catalogue record for this book is available from the British Library

ISBN: 978-1-138-48274-6 (Set)
ISBN: 978-0-429-42825-8 (Set) (ebk)
ISBN: 978-1-138-61780-3 (Volume 29) (hbk)
ISBN: 978-0-429-46147-7 (Volume 29) (ebk)

Publisher's Note
The publisher has gone to great lengths to ensure the quality of this reprint but points out that some imperfections in the original copies may be apparent.

Disclaimer
The publisher has made every effort to trace copyright holders and would welcome correspondence from those they have been unable to trace.

REPORT

ON

TRADE CONDITIONS IN CHINA

BY

HARRY R. BURRILL and RAYMOND F. CRIST
SPECIAL AGENTS OF THE DEPARTMENT OF COMMERCE AND LABOR

TRANSMITTED TO CONGRESS IN COMPLIANCE WITH
THE ACT OF FEBRUARY 3, 1905, AUTHORIZING
INVESTIGATIONS OF TRADE CONDITIONS ABROAD

WASHINGTON
GOVERNMENT PRINTING OFFICE
1906

CONTENTS.

SOUTHERN CHINA.

NORTHERN CHINA.

CONTENTS.

TRADE CONDITIONS IN SOUTHERN CHINA

By HARRY R. BURRILL

LETTER OF SUBMITTAL.

WASHINGTON, *May 10, 1906.*

SIR: I have the honor to submit herewith a report covering my investigation of trade conditions in China.

In accordance with instructions, my inquiries were especially directed toward the position occupied by the United States in the markets of the Empire and the steps necessary to insure a greater development of American commerce in the Far East. A careful study of the general conditions obtaining from Chefoo in the north to Hong-kong and Canton in the south indicates trade opportunities that no manufacturing country can well afford to ignore. If the exporters of the United States desire to participate in the benefits of the expansion, apparently inevitable within the next five years, they will find in the appended report some suggestions which, it is believed, will be of use.

Broadly speaking, up to this time only the surface of the trade with China has been scratched, but foreign importers are now gradually extending their business that they may reach the great consuming masses of the interior. The requirements of this vast market, now in the process of development, should be thoroughly investigated by American exporters with a view to manufacturing for the native millions the goods they demand at a price they can afford to pay.

It will require time and money to obtain the necessary technical details, but manufacturers for the export trade will find the expenditure a profitable investment, resulting, it is reasonable to assume, in the establishment of trade relations capable of enormous expansion.

Respectfully,

HARRY R. BURRILL,
Special Agent of the Department of Commerce and Labor.

The SECRETARY OF COMMERCE AND LABOR,
Washington.

11

SOUTHERN CHINA.

EXTENT AND POSSIBILITIES.

China, with its magnificent trade possibilities, has attracted the attention of the world, and manufacturing countries, anxious to participate in and benefit by its commercial growth, have carefully studied conditions with a view to exporting to the Orient the commodities required by the Chinese consumer. While in the last half-century gratifying progress has been made in the expansion of the world's trade with China, it is capable of demonstration that notwithstanding the efforts put forth the surface has thus far merely been scratched and that the opening of new territory, hitherto closed to commercial invasion, will blaze the way for the establishment, maintenance, and expansion of a vast business with the natives of the interior.

China is awakening, and, while the newly aroused national spirit contemplates the future control so far as practicable of the railway and waterway systems and other great enterprises for the development of her natural resources, it does not preclude nor does it discourage the advance of foreign commerce so long as it moves along legitimate lines. The trade of to-day is but a fraction of the figure it will eventually reach, for it is still restricted to the treaty ports, with of-course the natural movement of foreign commodities to the interior through Chinese merchants. Conditions now indicate that the period of exclusiveness, and to a greater or less degree suspicion and distrust, is passing, and that the natives in the distant provinces are beginning to realize that profitable business relations may be established with foreigners without causing them to lose "face," or in other words subject them to the contempt of their own race. To those who understand the Chinese character this is a distinct and significant gain in the exploitation of new commercial fields and the development of virgin territory, for it indicates that a breach has been made in the wall of native prejudice through which the army of commerce may now pass.

MASSES MUST BE CATERED TO.

According to the latest available statistics the population of the Chinese Empire approximates 432,000,000, of which possibly 3,000,000 constitute what may be termed the better class, including the nobility, literati, gentry, officials, and larger merchants. Slowly but none the less surely these Chinamen, representative of the intelligence, culture, and wealth of the Empire, have in a measure discarded their oriental narrowness and developed an appreciation of the merit of articles of foreign production. As a natural consequence the market for various commodities has expanded materially, but it is to the masses, numbering practically 430,000,000, that the manufacturers must cater in order fully to realize and enjoy the vast possibilities of the Chinese trade. Japan, Great Britain, Germany, and to a less extent other European countries, have recognized the necessity of studying the purchasing power and preferences of the poorer classes and of producing goods that can be laid down in China at prices within their reach. It must be admitted that American manufacturers have thus far paid too little attention to this exceedingly important phase of the trade with the Orient. If it be their desire and intention to compete successfully with the nations of Europe and with Japan, and assume their proper position in the trade conquest of China, they must defer to the whims, the prejudices, the likes, and the dislikes of the Chinese and abandon all efforts to force upon them commodities for which no demand can be created. By curbing the disposition to regard the Chinese Empire as a fit dumping ground for undesirable and unsalable goods American manufacturers and exporters can beyond question become important factors in the trade expansion of the near future.

IMPORTATIONS INCREASING.

It may be predicted with confidence, assuming that normal conditions prevail, that each succeeding year will show a substantial increase in the purchase of foreign-made goods by the masses of China, and a gradual expansion of the purchasing power of the poorer classes may with equal certainty be prophesied. The establishment of manufacturing plants in various parts of China has been largely instrumental in increasing importations, for with factories in operation the consumption is necessarily enlarged and more money is placed in circulation, all of which accrues to the benefit of exporting nations. Trade is stimulated by wealth-producing industries, and as China advances as a manufacturing nation, as she certainly will under the stimulus of successful ventures already made and the growing disposition to supply, in part at least, the demand for manufactured articles from her own factories, her trade relations with other countries will show a steady and consistent expansion.

AMERICANS NEGLECT OPPORTUNITIES.

The Empire, comprising one-twelfth of the land area and approximately one-fourth of the population of the globe, to a comparatively recent date has declined to enter into commercial intercourse with foreigners other than such as could not be avoided without working a hardship on her own people. Western ideas and methods by continuous assault on the trade gates of the Empire, barricaded by centuries of prejudice and distrust, have, however, at last broken down the defenses, and the last few years have been marked by extraordinary commercial development. In this all nations have participated, but the United States, by reason of her geographical position, should have benefited to a far greater extent than she has. As compared with European competitors, the American manufacturers are far more advantageously situated for placing their goods on the market of the Empire, but the expansion of our trade does not indicate that these advantages have been properly utilized. Wherever the fault may lie it is certainly not a difficult one to correct, and in view of the splendid trade opportunities presented it would be little short of a national blunder for our exporters to permit other countries to preempt this great commercial field and reap the golden harvest which energy, foresight, and preparedness would easily win for Americans.

IMPORTANCE OF EARLY ACTION.

American goods of all descriptions should be on the ground now, so that their distributors may be able to take advantage of the expansion of trade with the masses of the interior, that they may not be left at the post when this race for the great prize of the Orient really begins. It is of the highest importance to a manufacturing country that her products be among the first to command the attention of the Chinese consumer, for when a commodity has once been firmly established on the market and its standard is conscientiously maintained it is extremely difficult to dislodge it even though the article offered may be of superior quality and less expensive. The Chinese are peculiarly tenacious of their preference for an established "chop"' or trade-mark, which guarantees, or should guarantee, the quality of the commodity, and the manufacturer who disregards the integrity of his "chop" disappears as a factor in the trade, at least so far as that particular commodity is concerned. It is apparent, therefore, that in the development of new territory there should be no delay in the introduction of American wares. It is in fact a prime requisite to proper representation in the market, and any other method entails a long, tedious, and not infrequently unsuccessful, campaign against similar goods already firmly intrenched.

TREATY PORTS AND LIKIN.

There are certain fixed limitations under which foreign trade with China must be conducted and with which American manufacturers may be unfamiliar. Foreigners are not permitted to carry on business wherever they may desire in the Empire, and the restrictions are

fully as pronounced now as they were a decade ago.   True, through
the operation of treaties and other agencies, the number of treaty
ports has been increased to 36; some of these, however, are only partially opened to trade.   The Empire, generally speaking, is closed to
foreign commerce, and it is only at the following-named ports that a
foreigner may transact business:

Kiukiang.	Chungking.	Fuchau.	Kiaochau.
Wuhu.	Chinkiang.	Samshui.	Yochow.
Nankin.	Wenchow.	Lappa.	Changsha.
Ningpo.	Kongmoon.	Chingwantao.	Hankau.
Canton.	Kowloon.	Chefoo.	Hangchow.
Kiungchau.	Szemas.	Shasi.	Swatow.
Mengtsz.	Tientsin.	Soochow.	Pakhoi.
Tengyueh.	Ichang.	Amoy.	Lungchow.
Niuchwang.	Shanghai.	Wuchow.	Santuao.

Several of the largest and most important cities in the Empire are
not yet open to foreigners, but it is fair to assume, judging from the
present attitude of Chinese merchants and officials and the tendency
generally to commercial expansion, that within the next five years
large trading centers in the interior will be thrown open, affording more
direct business connections with the masses.

COST OF INTERIOR TRANSPORTATION.

It must be remembered, however, that goods entering an open port
are, generally speaking, subject only to a 5 per cent duty and afford
the provincial authorities practically no revenue whatever.   When
foreign goods are distributed from ports of entry to the interior, without a transit pass, and frequently in spite of the pass, they become
subject to likin, a native tax, unauthorized and indeed prohibited
under treaty regulations, but nevertheless in active operation along
the water transportation routes.   There is apparently no limit to likin
taxation, and, as a rule, the amount collected is as high as the traffic
will bear.   This condition affects the importer indirectly, but none
the less forcibly, for this addition to the cost of transporting goods to
the interior is finally paid by the consumer, and to that extent at least
lessens his purchasing power.

Under commercial treaty regulations importers may receive foreign
goods at the open ports, and after paying the 5 per cent duty may transship to the interior on the payment of an additional customs charge
of 2½ per cent.   This is called the transit-pass system and was designed
to supersede the likin tax, but it has proved ineffective so far as cor-
recting the abuse is concerned.   The Chinese shipper may pay the
additional 2½ per cent to the Imperial Maritime Customs, and armed
with his transit pass dispatch his goods inland, but at the first likin
barrier his shipment is probably held up until local authorities are

satisfied that they have relieved him of as much money as he can stand. The likin tax is one of the abuses of China which must of necessity gradually disappear, but until its complete suppression it will continue to constitute a serious menace to the expansion of trade with the interior.

INTERNATIONAL COMPETITION.

POSITION OF THE UNITED STATES IMPROVING.

The position of the United States with regard to trade in China is steadily improving, although possibly not with the rapidity which our natural advantages would warrant. Great Britain retains a commanding lead in commerce with the Chinese Empire, while Germany is steadily increasing her exports under the impetus of her unexcelled system of gathering and disseminating valuable trade information. Japan is another important factor, and it is predicted that within the next five years she will gain rapidly on her competitors for reasons explained elsewhere in this report.

The Monthly Summary of Commerce and Finance of the United States, December, 1905, shows that in our principal commodities the United States in 1905 exported to the Chinese Empire 121,390 barrels of flour, valued at $445,053, and to Hongkong, the great flour market of the Orient, 789,732 barrels, valued at $2,903,884; cotton piece goods, Chinese Empire, 562,732,721 yards, valued at $33,514,818, and to Hongkong, 455,675 yards, valued at $63,047; mineral oils, Chinese Empire, 76,968,639 gallons, valued at $6,485,587, and to Hongkong, 10,197,600 gallons, valued at $956,393.

COMPETING NATIONS.

For purposes of comparison, the latest complete figures available, indicating the value of imports into and the exports from the Chinese Empire for the years 1895 and 1904, are shown in the tables on page 19. The countries selected are the United States, Great Britain, Germany, France, Japan, and Hongkong. The necessity for including Hongkong is apparent, because although a British colony it is a port of entry and distributing center for enormous quantities of goods imported for Chinese consumption, and is separately designated in customs statistics. The percentage of increase in the value of American goods exported to China is 413 per cent, giving her in that respect a commanding lead over her principal trade rivals. While this percentage of increase shows a gratifying expansion, too much importance should not be attached to it, for in 1904 the total imports from the United States constituted only 9.8 per cent of the imports from the United States, Great Britain, Germany, France, Japan, and

Hongkong, as against 3.3 per cent in 1895. This is of course a healthful, and it might be called a vigorous growth, but all of our leading competitors show a large percentage of increase in their trade during the last ten years. With advantages of location second only to. Japan our commerce should have shown a far greater proportionate increase.

JAPAN AND GREAT BRITAIN.

Japan's trade with China has increased 161 per cent in the last ten years. With her emissaries scattered broadcast throughout the Chinese Empire spreading the gospel of Japanese trade advantages, and with a paternal government aiding in every way possible the commercial ventures of its subjects, it may be safely assumed that the next decade will show a wonderful increase in Japan's commerce with her neighbor. Great Britain, for years a dominating factor in the trade of the Far East, has increased her commerce with China during the last ten years 50.9 per cent. Conservative business methods, catering to the requirements of the trade, the popularity of her "chops," long established on the market, and energetic efforts to introduce her commodities are largely responsible for the expansion of her already splendid commerce. She is so strongly intrenched that her position would at first glance appear unassailable, but in the north she has been compelled to beat a partial retreat because of the constantly increasing importation of American piece goods. In the south, however, with Hongkong as a distributing point, English commodities make a remarkable showing, and their popularity may be a difficult but not by any means impossible task for American manufacturers to overcome.

GERMANY AND FRANCE.

The exports of Germany to China have steadily increased during the past decade by reason of her admirable system of gathering information valuable to German manufacturers and shippers and available only to German subjects, her careful attention to the needs of the market, her venture into the field of novelties, and her methods of disposing of her products. Germany's acquisition of a part of Shantung province has proved valuable in the expansion of her trade, and encouragement of a substantial character from the home Government has enabled German merchants in the Far East to prosecute their business enterprises along far less conservative lines than their trade competitors, with the possible exception of Japan.

While the imports from France show an increase in the last ten years of 155 per cent, the volume of trade is greatly restricted in comparison with the other countries under discussion. In 1895 she exported goods valued at $598,000, and in 1904 her exports amounted to $1,125,000. This comparatively insignificant showing is explained partially by the fact that France fails to manufacture goods suitable for Chinese consumption, though the increase in the last ten years would apparently indicate that she is slowly awaking to the needs of the market.

IMPORTS INTO CHINA IN 1895 AND 1904.

Imported from—	1895.	1904.	Increase.
			Per cent.
United States	$3,967,000	$20,368,000	413
Great Britain	26,455,000	39,940,000	50.9
Germany (including Hongkong)	8,428,000	*a* 12,578,000	49.2
France	598,000	1,525,000	155
Japan and Formosa	13,395,000	35,015,000	161
Hongkong	68,701,000	98,477,000	43.3

a In addition to the above figures, Germany exported in 1904 $1,708,000 to Hongkong and $1,801,000 to Kiaochau.

EXPORTS FROM CHINA IN 1895 AND 1904.

Exported to—	1895.	1904.	Increase.
			Per cent.
United States	$11,983,000	$18,907,000	57.7
Great Britain	8,235,000	10,658,000	29.4
Germany (including Hongkong)	4,401,000	*a* 8,173,000	85.7
France	26,480,000	34,427,000	30
Japan and Formosa	11,546,000	26,515,000	130
Hongkong	42,669,000	60,627,000	42.1

a In addition to the above figures, Germany imported in 1904 from Hongkong $46,000 and from Kiaochau $9,000.

INCREASE OF CHINA'S EXPORTS.

China's exports to the countries under discussion show in every instance a gratifying increase. It will be seen, however, that with the exception of France the balance of trade is against the Empire. The total value of imports into China for consumption in 1895, according to the Monthly Summary of Commerce and Finance of the United States, was $134,610,000 and in 1904, $240,154,000. The value of the exports from China in 1895 and 1904 was $112,341,000 and $167,162,000, respectively. This shows that the imports have increased 77.7 per cent during the last ten years and the exports 48.8 per cent.

NATIVE COTTON AND MANUFACTURES.

SUPERIOR QUALITIES—MARKETS SUPPLIED.

China produces large quantities of cotton, but it is mostly of inferior quality because of improper cultivation, and the native growers after selling their crop have a habit of adding foreign matter to the cotton, which increases the weight, but materially decreases the value. This is a common practice among the planters. Japan is the principal importer of Chinese cotton. From September, 1905, to January 7, 1906, there were exported from China to Japan 577,389 piculs (133⅓ pounds to a picul). The markets that buy cotton from China, in addition to Japan, are Antwerp, Bremen, Genoa, Hamburg, Havre, Hongkong, Liverpool, London, Kiaochau, Marseille, and Trieste. Tungchow cotton is the best produced by China and may therefore be designated as No. 1; Kajoa, No. 2; Taichong, No. 3; Shanghai, Nos. 4 and 5, and Ningpo, No. 6. Approximately 15 per cent of the total crop is consumed in China for the manufacture of yarn.

The total exports of native goods in 1904 amounted to $158,061,000, a creditable showing, but capable of enormous expansion if the masses of southern China could be imbued with a spirit of energy and ambition. In certain provinces there is unquestionably a discouraging feebleness of character due, it is charged by those thoroughly in touch with the situation, to opium and ignorance. It is difficult to comprehend how China, paying heavy indemnities and with her imports for years exceeding her exports, can stagger along under such adverse conditions, but she has demonstrated her power to do so in the past, and there appears to be no apprehension concerning her ability to do so in the future.

BUSINESS METHODS AND FINANCE.

THE CREDIT SYSTEM AND CASH SALES.

In discussing trade possibilities it is necessary to consider the constantly improving methods of transportation which will facilitate the movement of goods to the great masses of the interior and develop the natural resources and increase the purchasing power of the natives. We must also examine the business methods, banking, currency, the guilds, "squeeze," Chinese peculiarities and eccentricities, customs regulations and other limitations found in the prosecution of trade in order that our exporters may fully understand existing conditions.

The method usually employed by American exporters in transacting business with the importers at Chinese ports is cash against documents, which means practically a cash transaction, allowing the importer no opportunity to dispose of his cargo before he is obliged to pay for it unless ordered under a contract. Another system is for the home office to pay cash for the goods and draw a sixty or ninety days' sight draft on their representatives in China. The goods are under the control of the banks until the drafts are paid or satisfactory arrangements for their future payment are made. In the event of the failure of the consignee to take care of the draft the bank may dispose of the goods by auction or otherwise.

Credits are frequently extended by German exporters, which, it must be admitted, occasionally result in loss. The credit method, however, affords not only encouragement but accommodation to

German merchants in China and enables them to take greater chances with the market.

English exporters usually pursue a safe, conservative, course with their representatives. The usual method of financing orders is for Manchester, for instance, to draw upon Shanghai at from sixty days to four months sight, and in extreme cases six months sight, all depending on the standing of the merchant engaged in business. Interest at the rate of 6 per cent is added from the date of the bill to the date of return of the funds to England. As a rule a documentary credit is arranged on terms as above, with the banks doing an Eastern business. Under this system a merchant may make partial deliveries of goods shipped, the bank accepting pro rata payments. He is also permitted to retire his draft before the due date and interest will cease on the day he settles.

SALES FOR CASH.

Sales to the native merchants are usually made for cash except in infrequent cases, when the comprador of the importer guarantees the account, accepting full responsibility for its payment. Instances may be cited, however, where on the representation of a reliable native customer that he is temporarily short of cash and desires credit for a bill of goods, he has been accommodated with the result that he has met his obligation at the time specified. Commercial integrity is regarded as a valuable business asset by the Chinese merchants, and it is very rarely, barring unforeseen financial embarrassments, that he defaults in settlement and thus loses the confidence of his foreign and native trade associates. The guilds also help to maintain the solvency of the native merchants when they may be in temporary financial distress. The foreign business men of China regard the system now in operation as a good one, and while it may work a hardship in some cases it is apparently a safe and sound plan to follow.

FLUCTUATIONS IN CURRENCY.

The all-important money question of China has been so exhaustively investigated and explained by Professor Jenks, and his recommendations have met with such universal commendation, that it would be useless iteration to dwell on the subject in this report. It is sufficient to emphasize the great need of stability and uniformity in the interest of satisfactory commercial relations with China. The present system evidently commends itself to the Chinese, who, through its operation, are permitted almost daily to indulge in the luxury of speculation and exchange, a form of gambling dear to the heart of every true Chinaman. The fluctuations in the price of silver, the variations of taels, different districts having a different standard, and the complications in the coinage of copper cash—the money of the masses—are all a menace to the transaction of business along safe and conservative lines. In this connection it may be interesting to note the recent enormous increase in the importation of copper into China. This was due to the possibility of unrestricted coinage of copper pieces, an operation virtually under the absolute control of the provincial authorities. While the multiplicity of mints threatened the debasement of the currency of the Empire, the central Government until recently left the question of production entirely to the viceroys of the provinces.

The Shanghai Chamber of Commerce investigated this question and informed the diplomatic corps at Peking that representations looking to the regulation of currency should be made to the Government. The chamber pointed out that as the Chinese provincial governments imagine they have a perennial source of income from the profit of the mints they might fail to grasp the dangers of depreciation because of over-issue. It was further suggested that if restrictions were not established foreign trade in China must inevitably suffer. In the report on the Trade of China and Abstract of Statistics, it is estimated that the output for 1904 approximated 1,745,000,000 copper pieces, and the Shanghai Chamber of Commerce declared that by 1906 if all the mints, new and old, were in operation the output would reach in round numbers 16,413,000,000 pieces. There are eighteen or nineteen mints now in operation in China, but although bankers and merchants have given the subject close study they find it extremely difficult to obtain through unofficial channels absolutely accurate information as to their present producing power.

There is no uniformity in the value of "cash," for in some provinces 1,200 or 1,300 can be bought with a Mexican silver dollar, while in an adjoining province possibly 800 cash only are regarded as the equivalent of the silver dollar. The tael, approximately 1 ounce of silver, is the standard of value in the larger commercial transactions, and, while it is the principal standard by which the Chinese govern their business, its value varies, according to locality and the price of silver, creating embarrassing complications.

HAIKWAN TAEL.

The Imperial Maritime Customs of China, with a view to minimizing as far as possible the evils of the system, has adopted what is known as the haikwan tael for the payment of customs duties. The value of the haikwan tael is fixed arbitrarily at the beginning of each month and remains unchanged for that period, notwithstanding the fluctuations of exchange. While this plan unquestionably simplifies the business transactions of the importers, it can not be said to work any real or lasting benefit. As a matter of fact, during my stay in China the values of a haikwan tael and a Shanghai tael were never the same in any given month, the rates of exchange influencing from day to day the value of the latter while the value of the former remained stationary. An ingot of silver, worth approximately 10 taels, called the sycee, is frequently used in making large payments, and a shoe, so designated because of its resemblance to Chinese footwear, represents a value of about 50 taels. All are silver, however, subject to the vexatious and uncertain variations of exchange. The conditions of the monetary system consistently and insistently point to the necessity for its radical reform.

PROFITS OF FOREIGN BANKS.

The foreign banks make in the aggregate large profits out of their depositors alone—legitimately, it is true, under existing conditions, but in a way somewhat unsatisfactory to business men accustomed to the simpler methods encountered at home. If a merchant desires to convert gold into Mexican money, the bank will quite willingly accommodate him, retaining its commission first, for transferring the gold into taels; and second, for transferring the taels into Mexican money. Reversing the proposition, the bank is entitled to its two commissions, and the transactions, from the view point of a layman, bear a resemblance to that popular pastime of the Chinese known to the initiated as "squeeze," to which reference will later be made. With the exception of the International Banking Corporation, a banking institution doing business under a United States charter, there are practically no American banks in China. As a matter of fact, it was difficult to find an American official in the various branches of this corporation, the positions being filled by British employees so far as I was able to discover. By this, no reflection whatsoever is intended on their ability, their courtesy, or their willingness promptly to dispatch business, but the employment of American banking officials instead of foreigners in a distinctively American institution would have a tendency at least to uplift American prestige in the Far East and possibly introduce live, up-to-date business methods, where, it must be conceded, they are needed.

In view of the large profits made in exchange in the payment of the Chinese indemnities and in business transactions generally, it would be interesting to know just how the various banking corporations of the Orient view a reform in the money system of China. That they would favor a change appears doubtful when the extraordinary success of their operations is considered.

As an illustration, the Hongkong and Shanghai Banking Corporation may be cited. Its shares, having a par value of $125 Mexican, are now quoted on the markets of China at $900 Mexican. It has a reserve fund of $18,500,000, and its immensely valuable property throughout the entire East has been so persistently written off that it now stands on the bank books at the absurdly low valuation of $1,038,849. This bank pays 5 per cent on fixed deposits for a year and is regarded by conservative business men as one of the safest banking institutions in the world. Germany, France, Russia, Belgium, and Japan, as well as the United States, are also represented by banking corporations, all of which have profited enormously because of and not in spite of China's monetary system.

OPERATIONS OF EXCHANGE.

In a recent report H. B. Morse, an American occupying the position of statistical secretary of the Imperial Maritime Customs, discusses clearly and concisely the operations of exchange as applied to the Chinese Government, the importers, and the exporters. He writes in part as follows:

When the Chinese Government pays to the depository banks an installment of money on a due date, it is a popular belief that the silver so paid in is boxed and shipped in its original shape to the several powers in the proportion of their claims. The fact is that on the due date the Chinese Government becomes a buyer of bills for gold exchange. Now bills of exchange are like other commodities, the price depending on relative supply and demand. Importers of foreign goods buy exchange, paying here the silver they have received from selling the goods and receiving in foreign countries the equivalent in gold with which to pay the original cost; and exporters of native goods sell bills, receiving here the silver with which to buy the goods and repaying to the bank the proceeds of the sale in foreign countries. When the Chinese officials wish to buy exchange, they find that importers also wish to buy, and they both are competing for the bills to be sold by exporters. Suppose that on a given day the exchange is 7 taels for 1 pound sterling and that Chinese officials wish to buy bills for 1,000,000 taels and importers also wish to buy for 1,000,000 taels. If exporters on that day wish to sell bills for 2,000,000 taels, then the rate of exchange is unaltered, and the bank makes its profit from the difference between the buying and selling rates. But suppose exporters on that day have bills for 1,000,000 taels to sell, then the price goes up, as is the case always when demand exceeds supply. If the price goes up to, say, 8 taels for 1 pound sterling, the Chinese Government must still of necessity buy; perhaps half the importers must buy, while half may wait for more favorable exchange, and exporters who did not intend to sell bills at 7 taels may, if they can receive 8 taels, increase their sales from 1 million to $1\frac{1}{2}$ million taels.

NEW BANK NEEDED.

On the dates when indemnity installments are due, the rates of exchange almost invariably show a material increase, and this extra amount helps to swell the enormous profits of the banking corporations. American business men who are trading in China settle their exchange, and not an inconsiderable part of their profit finds its way into the coffers of foreign banking institutions. Business men of the Chinese Empire, who are not interested directly or indirectly in the prosperity of the banks, and who believe that their profits should be confined within reasonable limits, express the opinion that the establishment of a banking institution under proper regulations, whereby its notes would be redeemable at face value at any of its branches in the East, would be of vast benefit. If such a bank could be managed along the lines to which we are accustomed, eliminating practices legitimate perhaps, but expensive, and which would not be tolerated by the world of trade at home, they believe that the merchants of the Far East would gladly transfer their accounts to such an institution and insure its success from the start. This suggestion carries with it the incorporation of a bank with an American charter, manned by American officials with, of course, the necessary Chinese staff, and conducting business by American methods.

NATIVE BANKS.

Comparatively little is known of the practices of native banks. In order to facilitate modern trade, however, the rules regulating the banking system are less stringent than they formerly were, but they are still sufficiently strict to insure safety and, so far as they can be understood and intelligently discussed, have been commended by occidental banking experts. While there is no law in China governing the organization and incorporation of native banks, they are, when established, surrounded by such safeguards as to warrant confidence in their stability. There are comparatively few bank failures in China, for the reason, perhaps, that the Government metes out summary justice to those in control if it be shown that their carelessness, or worse, was responsible for the disaster. While their banking methods are probably more cumbersome than those of the West, they accomplish the purpose desired, doing it in a way that leaves small foundation on which to base a complaint and apparently meeting the necessities of native business.

POWER OF THE GUILDS.

In the prosecution of any business enterprise of whatever description in China the power and scope of the guilds must receive careful consideration. Thoroughly organized and managed, their membership including natives of a high order of intelligence, keen and alert to protect the interests of the members, they exert a controlling influence on trade. They are a recognized institution and an important factor in shaping commercial China.

The guilds are organized to protect, encourage, and promote the business interests of their members. A list of the various organizations would cover practically all the trade enterprises of the Empire. There are the Piece Goods Guild, the Tobacco Guild, the Jinrikisha Coolies' Guild, the Bankers' Guild, the Flour Guild, the Tea Guild, the Silk Guild, the Wheelbarrow Coolies' Guild, the Oil Guild, and various others, whose names are legion, corresponding in size and importance to the business enterprises which they are organized to foster and protect.

Under their constitution they are empowered to examine the books of a firm for the purpose of discovering, if there be any question raised, whether that particular firm has contributed its pro rata share to the support of the guild. This of course is applicable only to Chinese business houses, for foreign firms would never consent to such proceedings. A guild may also settle disputes over money matters between its members, and this appeal to arbitration has the effect of preventing many cases from being taken to the courts. Various other rules governing the business methods of the members are in force and must be complied with under penalty of fine or expulsion, either of which work almost irreparable damage to the business of the member so punished. Full and free discussions of all matters relating to the several business enterprises represented in the guild are regularly indulged in and no interest, however trivial, is neglected or overlooked. It will thus be seen that the guilds exert a tremendous influence in the commercial affairs of the Chinese Empire and that no enterprise is too large or small to feel the weight of their displeasure or enjoy the benefit of their approval.

ART OF BOYCOTTING.

The guilds are by no means novices in the art of boycotting, and have demonstrated, not infrequently, that to incur their enmity means commercial ruin. Their activity and rigid obstinacy in the American boycott indicated only too clearly their power, and it is safe to assume that they can tie up the business of any man, foreign or native, who runs counter to their wishes. It must be admitted in their favor, however, that their membership includes usually a majority of fair-minded and upright men who countenance a trade blow only when they believe themselves to be strictly in the right. The guilds, under normal conditions, can hardly be regarded as a menace to the successful operation of a business enterprise conducted by foreigners, for commercial relations between the foreign merchants and the native merchants, who are members of the guild, are so close that to disturb them would inevitably work an injury to both.

COMPRADOR SYSTEM.

Unusual methods are employed in trade in the Far East, and perhaps the strangest is the use of the comprador, a Chinese agent through whom business houses deal with the native buyers. Opinions differ as to the advantages of this system, but careful inquiry indicates that the large majority of foreign merchants regard the comprador as an indispensable adjunct to their business relations with the Chinese. The comprador has reached his present commanding position through a system of development difficult to comprehend when viewed through Western eyes. Originally his duties were confined to buying supplies in the native markets, engaging servants, and other unimportant work designed to relieve his employer from petty details. He is now, as years have developed the system, all-important, and American firms trading in the Far East can not afford to ignore or belittle his power. A comprador is primarily a cashier handling the money received by the firm and making the disbursements. His duties are, however, in reality far more comprehensive, embracing a general supervision of the purchase and disposal of various commodities to the Chinese, loaning or borrowing money for the firm with which he is connected, supplying money when needed, if he be a partner in the business, and protecting it from the various abuses which obtain in Chinese commercial circles. He engages and pays the Chinese staff and handles the native customers, who seldom have direct communication with the foreign members of the firm. Usually under a heavy bond for the faithful discharge of his duties, the comprador is a man of ability and good judgment, whose knowledge of the business standing of the natives transacting business with his firm enables him to protect it from loss. Constantly in touch with the native merchants, his acquaintance with the needs of the market enables him to discriminate between salable and unsalable goods and thus prevent unprofitable investments. His knowledge of the Chinese is invaluable to his employers or associates in business, and, because either his own money or that of his bondsman is involved, if for no other reason, the comprador may usually be regarded as a man of tact, judgment, and energy, disposed to pursue conservative business methods.

Complaints are heard that the comprador is generally a " grafter " in our common acceptation of the term. He is accused of " squeezing " both his employers and the Chinese purchasers in the transactions in which he acts as a go-between. He is charged with demanding payment from natives for employing them and then retaining a part of their monthly wage as his commission. His perquisites have gradually grown to large proportions, but, as a usual thing, they are not unknown to the firm with which he is connected, and as a matter of fact they are frequently recognized as part payment of the comprador's salary. Business men admit, moreover, that the usefulness of the comprador more than repays them for his peculations, if they may be so called, and it may be predicted that as an important factor in trade his position is unassailable for years to come.

INFLUENCE OF GRAFT.

Graft or " squeeze," as it is called in China, is not by any means confined to the compradors, for the practice is as prevalent among the natives as is ancestor worship. It is a recognized institution, annoying in the extreme to foreigners with their notions of honorable dealing and their contempt for petty theft, but if they transact business in

China they will have to grow accustomed to it. The size of the squeeze is not of so much importance to the Chinaman, although, of course, the larger the amount the better for his personal needs. It is the mere fact that he has made his squeeze that gratifies him. This practice prevails in every line of business, in the household, in short everywhere and under all conditions. The highest and the lowest, the richest and the poorest, all indulge, and it is through this well-known weakness of the Chinese character that lucrative Government contracts are obtained by those who understand and are willing to take advantage of the situation. While the Chinese could instruct the world in the finer points in the art of grafting, it must be remembered that in the Far East it is regarded in an entirely different light than elsewhere. The elimination of squeeze, entailing the overthrow of a popular national institution, would deprive Chinamen of a system of revenue which it has taken centuries of practice to bring to its present state of perfection.

With a Chinese comprador and shroff, who handles the petty cash, and the native staff necessary satisfactorily to transact business, the foreign merchant may expect a squeeze of some kind from the beginning of the year to its close, but the losses incurred are not of sufficient size to alarm those who may contemplate the establishment of a new business enterprise in China. These are items quite properly chargeable to profit and loss and they have apparently worked no lasting hardship on the foreign firms now trading in the Chinese Empire.

TREATY OBLIGATIONS AND CONCESSIONS.

ADMISSION OF FOREIGN GOODS—VALUE OF CONCESSIONS.

All foreign goods must enter China through the treaty ports, but this does not imply that all treaty ports are situated on the coast, for more than one-half of the cities, so classed, are to be found in the interior. There are now approximately thirty-five treaty ports so located as best to facilitate trade between China and foreign countries, and those remote from the coast are usually accessible either by the natural or artificial waterways with which China is abundantly provided. Trade privileges accompany the opening of treaty ports, and it is safe to assume that the favorable attitude of the Chinese Government toward granting such concessions indicates that it is not averse to the extension of commercial relations with foreign nations. At these ports the residents of foreign countries transact their business with the natives, and with these ports as a base foreign importers are gradually extending their trade to the interior through Chinese associates. These Chinese are, of course, permitted to transact business in cities, towns, and districts closed to foreigners, and under their contract may be relied upon to develop their especial line of trade to the greatest possible extent.

EXTRATERRITORIALITY.

Under treaty obligations China has surrendered her right to jurisdiction over the person and property of foreigners on her land and waters, and they are no longer subject to the operation of the Chinese law. China is still responsible, however, for the protection of foreigners, notwithstanding the fact that the laws of other nations are in force within her territorial limits. With extraterritoriality in operation in the various treaty ports of China the interests of foreigners are well safeguarded, and it renders under ordinary conditions the investment of money in business enterprises comparatively free from risk. However much natives might be disposed to harass foreign merchants—and there are many who still resent the presence of foreigners as inimical to their interests and a menace to the welfare of the Government—serious trouble is infrequent, and business may be conducted with as little danger of interruption or disturbance as in our own country.

Under the favored-nation clause the United States, and in fact all nations having treaty relations with China, exercise judicial power through their consular representatives, who, when sitting in a judicial capacity, preside over what is known as the "consular court." Thus it may safely be said that the personal rights and property interests of all Americans residing in treaty ports are carefully looked after on all occasions and fully protected when the necessity arises. The Chinese Government chafes at an obligation which destroys part of her sovereign rights, and yet holds her to as strict an accountability as if she were in possession of those rights; but in China extraterritoriality is essential to the preservation of amicable relations, and is so recognized by all nations enjoying privileges and exemptions under the favored-nation clause.

CONCESSIONS TO FOREIGNERS.

Treaty rights do not, of course, include an obligation on the part of the Chinese Government to grant concessions which enable foreigners to undertake the development of the vast natural resources of the Empire, and yet up to 1904 there was comparatively little difficulty experienced in investing capital in such enterprises, provided the proper authorities were approached in a proper way. Those opportunities were seized, and as a result railway, mining, and other valuable concessions were granted to foreigners, who in some cases conscientiously adhered to the terms of the contract and entered upon the work of development in a manner calculated to inspire confidence in the minds of the Chinese. Unfortunately, however, there were several marked exceptions where it became evident, not only to the native authorities but to observing foreigners as well, that the holders of concessions were absolutely indifferent to their specific obligations and were intent only on making money, regardless of right or justice.

It is useless to discuss these flagrant violations of agreement in detail, for they are too well known to require comment. Suffice it to say that they gradually created in the minds of the Chinese authorities and the masses the impression that they were victims rather than beneficiaries under the prevailing system of western "high finance," and they resolved, so far as practicable, to take matters in their own hands. To this end they have already bought back valuable concessions, entered into negotiations for the return of others, threatened to take possession forcibly, if necessary, of those whose owners decline to sell, and have resolved to grant no further concessions to foreigners. They declare openly that they intend to develop their own country, so far as lies in their power, and while the financial condition of the Empire will to a great extent necessitate foreign aid the Chinese are firm in their determination to retain in the future the control of such enterprises.

AMERICAN PRESTIGE CHECKED.

Probably one of the most valuable concessions ever granted by China was that of April, 1898, permitting American capitalists to construct a railroad between Canton, the important Chinese seaport of the south, and Hankau, the "Chicago of China," destined to be the greatest commercial center of the interior. The distance to be covered by the line was approximately 600 miles, passing through a rich agricultural section and tapping extensive coal and iron deposits. The highly productive interior to the west was tributary to the proposed road, and the enterprise was widely and justly regarded as one destined to preeminent success. To the Chinese its construction meant the rapid development of the splendid natural resources of the Empire, and no undertaking could have been started under more favorable auspices. The fiasco is history, and it dealt a serious blow to American prestige in China from which it will take many years to recover.

TRANSPORTATION.

RELATIVE ADVANTAGES OF ROUTES.

Freight rates and the time consumed in shipments of goods from American to Chinese ports are highly important factors in developing the markets. Competition is so keen between the products of American and European factories that the question of a few cents either way on the rate per ton exerts an influence that it might be difficult to understand at home. American manufacturers in order to be successful in the Chinese market must lay down their products at destination at a price that will enable them, if possible, to undersell, or at least to quote as low a price as the English, German, French, Dutch, or Japanese exporters. The American exporter has two routes to the Orient—one by the way of the Pacific coast and the other via the Suez

Canal. It may be said that either is acceptable to the importer, but preference is given to the line quoting the lower rate and permitting of the delivery of cargo at the earlier date. Rarely can the two be combined, and therein lies an opportunity for improvement that could not fail to be of advantage to both the manufacturers and the transportation companies. Reasonably low freight rates, quick delivery, and careful service can assist in the development of a market, and it is apparent that a harmonious and equitable arrangement between the shippers and transportation companies would result in increased trade.

For the information of manufacturers and as a basis for comparison between the Suez and Pacific-coast routes the tariffs for principal exports are submitted.

In shipments from New York local railway freight charges are not included. The rate from New York to Hongkong, Shanghai, Kobe, and Yokohama is the same, but the length of time required for shipments to reach their destination varies somewhat, and in the past has created some dissatisfaction among the importers of the Orient. There are, however, now in operation four lines between New York and the Far East, which run annually at equal intervals twenty boats to China and twenty to Manila and Japan. This plan should obviate the difficulties which have hitherto obtained regarding the uncertainty of the arrival of freight, for it permits the shipment direct to China or the delivery of goods in Japan without the delay occasioned by calling at Chinese ports after leaving Manila.

SUEZ ROUTE.

By the way of Suez from New York the freight rates on cotton piece goods per ton weight or measurement, at ship's option, are 22s. 6d.; general cargo (machinery, etc.), 32s. 6d.; on iron and steel products, plates, bars, rails, etc., from 20s. to 22s. 6d.; on oil, 30s.; on rosin, 27s. 6d.; on tobacco, $1.05 per 100 pounds, and on cigarettes, 55 cents per 100 pounds. Locomotives are shipped at a special rate approximating 35s.

In shipping to Tientsin, the rates on cotton goods are 15s. extra, and on general cargo 20s. extra.

The above list covers the principal articles exported from New York to the Orient via the Suez route, and the transportation companies have a schedule of sixty days to Shanghai.

CONTINENTAL ROUTE.

The following outward-bound through Asiatic tariffs apply via the Canadian Pacific Steamship Line, Great Northern Steamship Company, Nippon Yusen Kaisha, Northern Pacific Steamship Company, Boston Steamship Company, Boston Tow Boat Company, Portland and Asiatic Steamship Company, Occidental and Oriental Steamship Company, Pacific Mail Steamship Company, and the Toyo Kisen Kaisha, in direct connection with the Atchison, Topeka and Santa Fe, the Canadian Pacific, the Great Northern, the Northern Pacific, the Oregon Railroad and Navigation Company, the Southern Pacific, the Union Pacific, and their eastern connections to Yokohama, Kobe, Nagasaki, Moji, Japan; Shanghai, Hongkong, China. These rates apply to carload lots. Higher rates are charged for less than carloads.

Beef or pork, pickled or mess, in barrels from Chicago and defined territories West, $1 per hundred pounds; beer, etc., from all points, $1 per hundred pounds; bicycles, boxed or crated, all points, $3 per hundred pounds; bicycles completely knocked down and crated, all points, $2.45 per hundred pounds; boots and shoes, all points, $1.75 per hundred pounds; butter or butterine in hermetically sealed cans, all points, $1.50 per hundred pounds; candles, all points, $1.25 per hundred pounds; canned goods, all points, 90 cents per hundred pounds; cement in bags or barrels, all points, 75 cents per hundred pounds; copper in bars or ingots, from Montana, 55 cents per hundred pounds; from Michigan, 60 cents per hundred pounds.

Cotton piece goods.—Any of the following-named articles, made wholly of cotton, when specific name of the article and name of shipper are plainly marked on outside of packages and stated in shipping order or bill of lading (marking or describing packages as containing "cotton piece goods" will not be sufficient), viz, calicoes, cambrics, glazed, flat (not including tracing cloth), canton or cotton flannels, cottonades, cotton crash, cotton prints, cotton damask, cotton jeans, cotton plush, cotton dress linings, cotton dress goods of domestic manufacture in the original piece, cotton warp, cotton duck (not otherwise specified), buckram, cotton shirtings, canvas, denims, drills, domestic checks, stripes, and cheviots, domestic ginghams, sheetings, silesias, ticking, and scrims:

All points in State of New York and New England States, per 40 cubic feet.. $11.25
All points, except points in State of New York and New England States (expires
June 30, 1906), per 100 pounds in carload lots............................ 1.10
All points, except points in State of New York and New England States (effect-
ive July 1, 1906), per 100 pounds in carload lots....................... 1.25
Buffalo, S. C. (expires June 30, 1906), per 100 pounds in carload lots........ 1.19
Buffalo, S. C. (effective July 1, 1906), per 100 pounds in carload lots........ 1.34
Cotton, raw, machine compressed in square or round bales, minimum carload
weight 20,000 pounds, all points (rate includes compressing charge), per 100
pounds in carload lots... 1.35
Cotton waste, machine compressed in bales, minimum carload weight 24,000
pounds, all points, per 100 pounds in carload lots........................ 1.35
Cotton-seed meal, minimum carload weight 40,000 pounds (carried by special
arrangement only), all points, per 100 pounds in carload lots.............. .75

Iron or steel, all points, 60 cents to 75 cents per hundred pounds, according to weight of piece; lard, all points, 85 cents per hundred pounds; leather, in rolls or bundles, all points, $10 per 40 cubic feet or in boxes or cases $1.25 per hundred pounds; liquors, all points, $1.15 per hundred pounds; machinery, all points, from 95 cents to $2.20 per hundred pounds, according to weight; milk, condensed or malted, all points, 75 cents per hundred pounds; oil, all points, 80 cents per hundred pounds; paper, all points, 52 cents per hundred pounds; pipes and fittings, all points, from 60 cents to 90 cents per hundred pounds, according to diameter; rails, Chicago and common points, $9 per ton, 2,240 pounds; sewing machines, all points, $1.25 per hundred pounds; soap, all points, 80 cents per hundred pounds; sugar, all points, $1 per hundred pounds; tobacco, manufactured, all points, $1.25, and unmanufactured from $1.50 to $1.75 per hundred pounds.

ARBITRARIES ON GENERAL CARGO.

The arbitraries on general cargo beyond Asiatic common points, applying via Hongkong, are as follows (the rates including 60 cents gold per ton for transshipping charges):

Port.	Arbitrary.	Minimum charge from Hongkong.	Port.	Arbitrary.	Minimum charge from Hongkong.
Amoy (China)	$2.50	$0.50	Macao (China)	$2.40	$0.50
Canton (China)	2.85	.50	Swatow (China)	2.00	.50
Cebu (P. I.)	3.50	1.00	Taiwanfoo (Formosa)	4.25	.50
Fuchau (China)	4.00	.50	Tamsui (Formosa)	4.25	.50
Haiphong (China)	2.50	.50			

The arbitraries to points beyond Shanghai are as follows (the rates including $1 gold per ton for transshipping charges at Shanghai):

Port.	Arbitrary.	Minimum charge from Shanghai.	Port.	Arbitrary.	Minimum charge from Shanghai.
Chefoo (China)	$3.00	$0.75	Ningpo (China)	$2.00	$0.75
Chinkiang (China)	2.25	.75	Taku (China)	4.75	.75
Hankau (China)	3.50	.75	Tientsin (China)	4.75	.75
Kiukiang (China)	3.50	.75	Weihaiwei (China)	3.00	.75
Kiaochau (China)	3.00	1.00	Wuhu (China)	3.00	.75
Niuchwang (China)	3.25	.75			

Shipments of cement, timber, and heavy weights for which special arrangements have to be made, should not be contracted beyond Shanghai, China, at a through rate of freight.

At the option of steamship lines freight destined to points for which arbitraries are provided via Shanghai, China, may be transshipped at Kobe, Japan.

The ports of Tientsin, Taku, and Niuchwang, China, are closed during December, January, and February, and Niuchwang is closed also during March. No shipments to be contracted which will arrive at port of transshipment during the months named.

The arbitraries to points beyond Yokohama are as follows (the rate including transshipping charge at Yokohama):

Port.	Arbitrary.	Minimum charge from Yokohoma.	Port.	Arbitrary.	Minimum charge from Yokohama
Hakodate, Japan	$2.50	$1.00	Tokyo, Japan	$1.00	

The freight rates from Manchester to Shanghai average 40s. to 46s. per ton, ship's option as to measurement. It will thus be seen that our exporters have an advantage over the Manchester mills in freight charges on goods destined for China, but a comparison of the trade in the Chinese markets in American and Manchester made commodities would apparently indicate that other conditions have interfered to prevent our home manufacturers from realizing to the fullest extent the benefits of a lower rate.

GERMAN LINES.

The German mail steamship lines are subsidized, but in order to collect the subsidy they must make schedule time at the various ports

29846—06——3

of call. Unless they do so they are penalized, and the result is, barring accidents, the arrival of German cargoes in the Orient can be estimated almost to a day. This is of great benefit to German traders, for it enables them to assure their customers that they can depend on the delivery of an order at a certain time, and it is infrequently that delays are reported. If, for instance, a Chinese merchant requires goods which are made in both the United States and Germany, and from the importer of the German commodity receives the unqualified promise of delivery within sixty days and from the dealer in the American goods an assurance of delivery at some indefinite future date, it is not difficult to see where the order will be placed. The importer of the American product may expatiate on the excellence of the make and its superiority in point of durability to the German article, but the Chinese buyer, knowing the needs of the market, requires a quick delivery on schedule time, and the fact that the German goods may be of inferior quality receives, broadly speaking, but little consideration from him.

DELAYS VIA SAN FRANCISCO ROUTE.

From San Francisco the Pacific Mail Steamship Line has its schedule for points in the Orient, and usually lives up to it, but vexatious and on their face apparently inexcusable delays in the arrival of cargoes were brought to my attention by merchants of Shanghai and Hongkong. Ships on this line having goods consigned to Chinese ports have not infrequently run counter to their schedule and sailed direct from Japan to Manila, cutting out the Chinese ports of call on the outward trip. It is true that on these occasions the officers of the liner have made efforts to transship the cargo destined for China at Yokohama, but this plan was unsatisfactory to the consignees, for it caused more or less delay at Yokohama, and instances have been reported where only a part of the consignment was transferred, the remainder going around by Manila and reaching its destination on the arrival of the Pacific Mail liner homeward bound. No doubt there were good reasons for this action, but it was none the less exasperating to the importers and harmful to trade.

JAPANESE AIMS.

Much has been written recently concerning the intention of the Japanese ultimately to control in part the transportation facilities of the Pacific. That negotiations are on foot appears to be assured, but until some definite action be taken it is useless for the purposes of this report to speculate on the consequences. With regard, however, to the coastwise trade of China, it is apparent that Japan has entered the field with a determination to control it. The Japanese openly declare, according to the shippers of various ports, that they will carry freight cheaper than any other lines, even though the transaction results in a loss in order eventually to break down competition. They now have boats in sufficient numbers to handle all the coastwise business, and as they are assisted by a subsidy from the Japanese Government it seems reasonable to suppose that ultimately their purpose will be accomplished. Two years ago the Douglas Line was operating at a profit eight coastwise steamers. The company has withdrawn all but three, and these, it is reported, are running at a loss because of Japanese competition.

COMMERCIAL CENTERS.

The various treaty ports of the Empire are to-day the commercial centers for merchants of all nationalities, among whom competition is noticeably keen for the establishment and maintenance of trade with the natives of the interior. The enormous volume of interior trade has in the past been handled with remarkable ease by means of the vast natural waterways and system of artificial canals and creeks. Innumerable native craft, heavily laden and operated by cheaper labor than can perhaps be found anywhere else on earth, transport goods to the far distant interior at a comparatively small expense to the dealer. Water transit is cheaper than land transportation, and with time an unrecognized factor among the natives in the ordinary transactions of life these cumbersome, slow-moving junks are as a rule regarded no whit inferior to the faster-going steam craft and certainly more economical. The advent of the railway, yet in its infancy, is to a certain extent effecting a wholesale change in the methods of transportation, and thus bringing the natives of distant provinces in closer and more frequent touch with the centers of distribution. Where sections of the country are inaccessible by water, goods are carried by junk as far as possible through this elaborate system of waterways and are then entrusted to coolies for transportation to their destination.

NATIVE COMMON CARRIERS.

A Chinese coolie may appropriately be called a beast of burden, docile and possessing remarkable endurance, and his services are utilized to the fullest extent in transporting merchandise. His work is done either by means of bamboo poles slung between barrows grouped in pairs, or in case of heavier weight by the wooden wheelbarrow, which is loaded to its fullest capacity, and on the weight of the goods depends the number of coolies employed to push and pull the burden. It is obvious that the wheelbarrow can not be comfortably operated in mountainous districts, and for this purpose the pack mule, pony, or donkey is utilized. Whatever may be the method employed by the Chinese in the transportation of goods from distributing points to the distant consuming markets, complaints are infrequent of loss or damage in transit, and no more time is consumed than was a thousand years ago, and what satisfied their ancestors is good enough for the Chinese of to-day. The Chinese craft is usually the home of the owner and his family. They have no other habitation, and as all bear a hand in the work necessary in transporting goods it becomes a family affair, and explains in part the cheap rate obtainable by the shippers. Another important factor is the keen competition, which in China as elsewhere has a tendency to lower prices.

RIVER TRANSPORTATION.

Lines of steamers ply regularly on the Yangtze River as far as Ichang and, when the depth of water permits, beyond that point. Boats leave Shanghai and Hankau every day in the week except Sunday, and are usually taxed to their full capacity both for freight and passengers. From the coast they carry to the interior imported goods for which there is comparatively urgent need, and from points along that great waterway they gather up products destined for export to all parts of the world. These steamship lines are under British and Chinese control, and while the competition is keen the difference in freight rates is so slight as to suggest at least amicable relations between the rival companies. Between Shanghai and Hangchow and Shanghai and Soochow there is steam communication, and also between Hangchow and Soochow, two large and commercially important cities, both rather inclined to an antiforeign sentiment. Between Hongkong, the great port of entry for southern China, and Canton and points beyond on the West River steamship lines run regularly, having boats in abundance to handle the enormous passenger and freight traffic of that territory. To points inaccessible for steamboats other means of transportation are found. The rates demanded by the coolies of the southern provinces are somewhat higher than those of central and northern China.

COMMUNICATION WITH THE INTERIOR.

It will be seen that there are comparatively few difficulties attending transportation from the coast to the interior, and that they would offer no impediment to the successful extension of trade relations with natives living hundreds and possibly thousands of miles distant, provided there were no mistakes made in properly introducing the goods and subsequently in maintaining the quality fully up to the standard of the first shipment. The railroads already built in China have borne an important part in the development of the trade with the interior, and it is safe to assume that the construction of railway lines now contemplated under Chinese control will prove of inestimable benefit to both the import and export trade of the Empire. The Chinese now control the lines from Paoting-fu to Peking; from Peking to Tientsin, and from Tientsin to Shanhaikwan and Niuchwang, covering a distance of approximately 300 miles and tapping rich, populous, and progressive provinces. They also own and operate 65 miles of railroad in Hunan province connecting the Pinghsaing with the Siang River, a road of 11 miles to the Tayeh mines, and the Fatshan division of the Canton and Hankau railway, approximating 30 miles.

RAILWAY CONSTRUCTION.

Up to the time of my departure from China these four railway lines, covering about 405 miles, were all that were under the control of and operated by the Chinese, but plans were well underway for the construction of new lines, upon which work is to be begun as soon as the capital necessary to finance them can be obtained. Railway officials, both native and foreign, connected with the Imperial Chinese Railway Administration, confidently predict that within a comparatively short time railway construction will have so far advanced as to be of practical aid in the development of the great natural resources in which China abounds. When transportation facilities can be had for the products of her vast coal fields, both bituminous and anthracite, an important problem will have been solved in the operation of factories and manufacturing enterprises generally. Instead of having to depend on Japanese coal for fuel, it will be possible to draw on the rich deposits of the Empire with a material reduction in cost and a saving in time. That this will be an important factor in stimulating the various new manufacturing industries already under consideration is regarded as assured, for the railroads thus far constructed have demonstrated in China, as they invariably have in other parts of the world, their usefulness in the development of industrial enterprises. The operation of these roads has also served to increase business, and since their construction there has been noticeable a slight expansion of the purchasing power of the natives.

GOVERNMENT OWNERSHIP AIMED AT.

Chinese railroad officials are assured that the railroads projected can easily be put on a paying basis, and it is the desire of the Government to develop these enterprises along the lines adopted in Japan, which would mean practically government ownership. It is the avowed intention of the Chinese to construct their own railways in the future, and in pursuance of this policy no further concessions will be granted. If they can not raise the money necessary to prosecute the work themselves, their plans, already matured so far as is possible without entering into actual negotiations, contemplate the engagement of some railway construction company to build the road for which work it is to be paid outright. The Chinese Government intends that the construction company shall have no interest in the completed line other than as mere contractors, and that the control and operation of the road shall be vested exclusively in the Government.

FOREIGN OWNERSHIP.

The Belgians now control the 650 miles of railroad between Hankau and Paoting-fu, traversing the rich provinces of Hupeh, Honan, and Pechili and connecting Paoting-fu with the railroads extending northeast to Niuchwang and operated by the Imperial Chinese Railway Administration. The equipment of the Belgian road, as might be expected, was obtained from Belgium, just as the equipment of the Hankow and Canton railway might have been imported from the United States, had not that line passed from the ownership of American capitalists into Chinese hands. Great Britain controls the railroad running from Woosung to Shanghai, a distance of 11 miles, and also the Nanziang division of the Shanghai-Nankin Railway, now having about 10½ miles in operation. It is expected that the Shanghai-Nankin Railway will have completed its division to Soochow, a distance of 65 miles, by June of this year. The growing sentiment among the Chinese in favor of railway construction indicates a radical departure from the narrow, commerce-paralyzing prejudices of centuries and the dawn of an era of trade expansion difficult to comprehend by those unfamiliar with the vast resources of the Empire. In this expansion the American manufacturers should be ready to participate, and in this report are pointed out the steps necessary to accomplish that purpose.

In the development inevitable with the newly aroused commercial spirit the exporters of the United States will have only themselves to blame if they fail to extend to gratifying proportions their business relations with the Empire. This, of course, presupposes the ultimate abandonment of the boycott movement and the return to normal conditions.

PERSONAL REPRESENTATIVES.

IMPORTANCE AND VALUE OF RESIDENT AGENTS.

China, with normal conditions restored, presents trade opportunities so vast and so remunerative that an investigation of the possibilities should move American manufacturers, exporters, and merchants to extraordinary efforts to obtain the share that rightfully belongs to them. They have natural advantages which, if properly utilized, will be of great assistance in the expansion of our trade, but they must go after the business for it will never seek them, and now is the time to do it. In this connection a few suggestions relative to the requirements of the markets of the Orient and the methods best calculated to insure business success are pertinent.

The testimony of business men and a careful investigation of existing and prospective trade conditions demonstrate clearly that personal representation is the keynote of success. An American manufacturer desiring to establish his particular line in the markets of China should intrust his business to a competent, experienced, and practical American whose own interests are so closely identified with those of his employer that every effort will be directed toward the expansion of trade.   The push, enterprise, and ability, inseparable from business success at home, should at all times characterize his work in China and live up-to-date American methods should at all times prevail. Samples are useful and necessary in many instances, but a stock of goods is infinitely preferable.   The Chinese merchant wishes a "look see," and if he finds what he wants at a price he can afford to pay the transaction is ended then and there by the delivery of the goods and payment therefor in cash.   In large orders the forward contract is essential, but this would in no way conflict for the samples carried by the American representative would enable the Chinese buyer to make his selection and contract for the delivery of the goods at a future date.   The Chinese naturally wish to see the goods they are purchasing, and catalogues, unless printed in both English and Chinese, and with full explanations of the cuts, are just about as useful as the fifth wheel of a coach.   Furthermore, the Chinese buyer wants to know what an article will cost in dollars and cents, and to show him a list price with the explanation that there will be an allowance of 40, 10, and 5 off enlightens him quite as fully as a passage from the Greek Testament would a Sioux Indian.

AMERICAN AGENTS NEEDED.

In the exploitation of new fields and the opening up of new territory the personal representative would be on the spot ready to take advantage of every opportunity presented.   It is safe to assume that a live American, backed by a house that executed his orders promptly and carefully, would be in the advance guard of commercial invasion. With the power to expend money judiciously for advertising purposes and to form commercial alliances with trustworthy Chinamen in order to promote trade with the natives of the interior, his usefulness would be evident from the start and would increase as time passed.   Is it not reasonable to suppose that an American agent would represent American goods far more satisfactorily than an Englishman or a German?   In the various treaty ports of China may be found British and German firms representing American manufacturers simply for the reason that there are no Americans there to act in that capacity.   In addition to handling American goods these English and German firms sell similar goods, manufactured in England and Germany, respectively, and there can be no uncertainty as to what commodities will be pushed.   By this no reflection is intended, for my experience with the foreign merchants of the Far East demonstrated their scrupulous regard for business integrity, but human nature is much the same the world over, and with every intention of affording equal opportunity the Englishman will, if he can, sell English goods, the German will sell German goods just as the American would, under similar conditions, sell American goods.

CLOSE TOUCH WITH MARKET.

Another important point in favor of a personal representative is his ability to keep in close touch with the market, and by so doing inform his employer promptly and in detail of the requirements of the native consumer. We must give the Chinese what they want and not what we think they should want. An agent on the ground would know what goods would be salable and what could not be disposed of however favorable might be the price and superior the quality. It may be set down as an incontrovertible fact that American manufacturers must cater to the Chinese trade and any other method will, in the majority of cases, result in complete failure. At best only partial success could result from the most determined attempt to force goods on the market. American manufacturers are careless in filling orders according to specifications, a fault that should be remedied at once. The importer in China enters into a contract with the native buyer to supply him with certain goods made in a certain way at a certain price. Complaints are frequent that the exporter fails to ship the goods according to the instructions received from his representative in China, and the result is not only a loss on that particular consignment but it creates in the mind of the Chinese buyer a feeling of distrust and suspicion extremely difficult to remove. One such mistake is far more harmful to trade than it is possible for our home manufacturers to realize, and the slightest deviation from specifications should always and under all circumstances be avoided.

ADHERENCE TO CONTRACT.

The terms of the contract entered into between their representative in China and the native merchant as to the time of delivery should always be carried out. The importance of this can not be overestimated, for upon the prompt arrival of the cargo depends the ability of the importer to keep faith with his customer, retaining in that way his confidence. It should certainly not take the manufacturer at home any great length of time to ascertain, after receipt of an order, whether he can fill it according to specifications and at the time required. If it can not be done, he should at once cable his representative to that effect and thus avoid unpleasant complications. A case, one of many brought to my attention which might be cited, indicated unpardonable carelessness on the part of the home manufacturers. A consignment of goods had been ordered for delivery on or about January 15. Ample time had been allowed for the manufacture and shipment, either by the Pacific coast or Suez, and the exporter had accepted the contract with a full understanding of its terms. On January 12 a cable was received by the representative in China announcing that one-half of the order would be delivered about March 1 and the remainder might be expected six weeks or two months later. The explanation vouchsafed was the demand of the home market, which kept the factory busy to the exclusion of foreign trade. It is not difficult for a business man to realize how grave a menace such contempt for ordinary fair dealing is to our commercial relations with China.

MARKETS SHOULD BE HELD.

The home market is evidently of sufficient size to consume, in many instances, the output of our factories, but if our manufacturers attempt to develop an export trade only to neglect it when the home demand is great enough to keep their factories running full time in order to supply it, the result is too obvious to require discussion. By declining to fill an order from China because by so doing they would jeopardize a sale at home American manufacturers not only lose that particular Chinese customer, who has placed his order with their representative, but they endanger all future transactions in that especial chop, for it is certain that their action will become known and widely criticized among the native merchants. No greater mistake could be made than to use the Chinese market as a makeshift, and any manufacturer of the United States might as well abandon the field if he enters it with that purpose in view. The development of the markets of China depends on the ability of the importer to supply within a reasonable time the demands of the native consumers, and this is impossible if the mills at home decline to entertain orders because of temporarily heavy sales in the United States.

PACKING.

LESSONS THAT SHOULD BE STUDIED.

Why American shippers should be so indifferent to the importance of proper packing is difficult to understand. Goods shipped from the United States to China frequently arrive in such a condition as to render them wholly or in part worthless, and this is largely attributable to carelessness in not affording sufficient protection against the rough handling incident to the railway and steamship journey. In practically every report dealing with special commodities that I have transmitted attention has been called to the careless methods of packing, but this vital mistake can not be too strongly or too frequently emphasized if we desire to maintain and develop the markets of China. Shippers should take into consideration the necessity for packing of great strength and durability when goods are consigned to a market

10,000 miles away. The protection afforded for a short or long railway haul within the limits of the United States is entirely insufficient to land them in China in an undamaged condition, and the sooner this fact is realized and acted upon the better it will be for our trade in the Orient. Attention has been directed to the best methods of packing various commodities, and those suggestions were based on the experience of practical business men who have suffered inconvenience and loss through the neglect of the manufacturers at home.

EUROPEAN METHODS.

The English manufacturers and the shippers of continental Europe have to a gratifying degree solved this important problem, and their goods, especially those from Great Britain, reach their destination in a satisfactory condition. In the past, when the packing of their goods was insufficient properly to protect them in their long journey, the shippers were so informed by their representatives in China and they promptly adopted improved methods. That one precaution alone has strengthened them wonderfully in the markets of the Orient, and it is inexplicable that our exporters do not act with equal promptitude and business sagacity on the recommendations of their agents. A Chinese merchant now knows that goods ordered from Europe will, barring accident, reach him in a satisfactory condition, and he is quite as well aware that he takes long chances on American shipments. Losses by damage are of course made good, but that has no bearing on the question. If the goods shipped from the United States were adequately packed, there would be comparatively few instances where damage would be sustained, and vexatious complications arising out of appraisements and settlements would in a great measure be avoided.

TRANSPORTATION COMPANIES NOT BLAMELESS.

In this connection it must be admitted that the method of handling goods by the transportation companies should be improved. More care ought to be exercised by both the rail and steamship lines, which are unquestionably responsible in part, at least, for the arrival in China of goods in a damaged condition. Although this difficulty could be minimized by more careful packing this affords no excuse for improper and careless handling of freight. Complaints are frequent too that delays often occur in transshipment at the Pacific or Atlantic coast ports, which render it impossible for importers to make deliveries at the time named in the contract, constituting another element of danger to our trade. Exporters and transportation companies are both vitally interested in the maintenance and development of our trade with China, and it seems incomprehensible that they should neglect any precaution calculated to promote it.

PORT REGULATIONS.

METHODS AND EXPENSE OF DISCHARGING CARGOES.

Shanghai is the principal port of entry and the great distributing point for northern and central China, especially for goods manufactured in the United States. The methods governing imports and reexports at this port are therefore of particular interest to American manufacturers, exporters, and merchants who may contemplate introducing their products into the Chinese market, and the information may also be of value to our producers who are already represented in the Far East.

While the Woosung bar, about 12 miles from Shanghai, can not now be crossed by many of the larger ocean-going steamers, it is hoped that the dredging operations soon to be begun will eventually remove that barrier and permit craft of all sizes and descriptions to anchor in the harbor. This will be of incalculable value to the commerce of Shanghai. When possible the ocean-going steamers discharge their cargoes at the godowns (warehouses) of the Shanghai and Hongkew Wharf Company (Limited), or those of the China Merchants Steam Navigation Company, which are situated on both the Shanghai and Pootung sides of the Whangpoo River. When steamers are too heavily laden, however, to cross the bar at Woosung, the whole or a part of the cargo is discharged into lighters and by them brought up to the godowns at Shanghai. No extra charge is made to the importer for this service for his goods in accordance with his bill of lading are to be delivered at "the port of Shanghai."

LANDING AND STORING GOODS.

The princip l premises of the Shanghai and Hongkew Wharf Company extend for over a mile along the Shanghai bank of the river, and there goods are placed if the consignees intend to take delivery within the ten-day free-storage limit. If not the goods are removed to the company's more substantial warehouses, where they are allowed to remain until delivery is taken. For goods so stored landing accounts are issued free unless the storage is under 5 mace, when an initial charge of that amount will be imposed for the first month. Renewal landing accounts are charged for at the rate of 1 tael each. The company is not responsible for the value of any package exceeding 250 taels, unless so declared on application for storage, nor for loss or injury of any merchandise by fire, typhoons, floods, effect of climate, or other "acts of God." Furthermore, the company takes no cognizance of the contents of packages nor of the condition of any merchandise received into their godowns. Packages with declaration of value are taxed half of 1 per cent. Consignees are allowed free storage for a period of ten days from the time the steamer arrives, the day of arrival being counted as one day. No charges are ever reckoned for a portion of a month; a whole month's storage is charged even if the goods remain but one day.

CUSTOMS DUTIES.

The customs duty amounts to about 5 per cent on all importations. There are, of course, exceptions to this rule, but the variation is so slight that it is safe to figure on 5 per cent as covering the customs charges. Upon the payment of this duty the goods are permitted to enter the port and are delivered to the consignee. On the arrival of the steamer carrying the cargo the consignee sends his bill of lading, which he has previously indorsed, to the agents of the steamer for counter signature—that is, a number corresponding to the manifest number is placed on the face of the bill of lading and it is stamped "deliver upon indorsement" and signed by the steamship agents. A clause is also stamped on the document to the effect that no claims for damage will be recognized after a certain date, usually fourteen days from the time of arrival of the steamer. The usual import application is then filled out and signed by the consignee. The importer is required to wait a day before he can obtain his duty memoranda. This document is made out in Chinese, but bears in English the name of the importer, name of the steamer, and amount of duty to be levied, in haikwan taels, together with the amount of the wharfage dues, also in haikwan taels. These dues amount to one-half of 1 per cent of the duty leviable. The duty memoranda and bill of lading are then presented at the customs bank, together with what is known as the pass book (bearing particulars similar to those on the import application), and the duty in haikwan taels is converted into Shanghai taels, and when paid a receipt in Chinese is given to the importer. A check on a local foreign bank is not accepted by the customs bank in payment of duties. In the case of small amounts silver or bank notes are accepted, but for large amounts the most convenient method of payment is to get a comprador order (in Chinese) from the comprador of the Hongkong and Shanghai bank, which he gives in exchange for a check on the same bank.

DELIVERY AND TRANSSHIPMENT.

As regards the delivery of goods from the wharf godowns, if it is desired to take delivery of the entire lot called for on the bill of lading that document is surrendered and the goods removed. If within the free-storage limit of ten days, no storage is charged, but if that time limit is exceeded by only one day one month's storage is charged. If, on the other hand, the importer has no storage facilities of his own and desires to leave his goods stored in the wharf godowns, the wharf company issues a landing account, a document showing the marks of the goods, description, etc., and on what date storage commenced, and the rate charged. Blank delivery order books are also issued by the wharf company, and when the importer desires to take delivery of a portion of his cargo one or more of these forms is filled out, and upon presentation at the wharf office the goods called for are delivered. Goods so stored are at owner's risk, and he must effect fire insurance if he so desires.

If the goods are shipped to a foreign port in China, such as Hong-kong, Wei-hai-wei, or Tsingtau, or to a foreign country, they are shipped under "drawback certificate;"—that is, within approximately three weeks from the time of shipment a drawback certificate is issued by the customs to the shipper for the amounts of duty paid on impor-tation. This certificate may either be cashed or used as legal tender in the payment of further duties. In the case of reexports by junk, towed by steam launches to ports like Soochow and Hangchow, a second duty is collected at destination, but drawback certificates are issued in Shanghai for the amounts so collected.

On shipments to interior points by native junk, a half duty is col-lected, in addition to the full duty paid upon importation. For this payment goods are supposed to be freed of all further taxation at native customs barriers en route. Cargo which has already been passed at the customs for reexport or transshipment may be reexported or transshipped again within three days free of duty, but is subject to examination by the customs examiners.

TRADE CENTERS.

PRINCIPAL POINTS FOR DISTRIBUTION.

Hongkong is the principal port of entry and the great distributing center for southern China, but it is impossible to obtain a classification of origin or the quality or value of goods imported from a particular country for the reason that Hongkong authorities are naturally unwilling to open their books for the inspection of officials of other governments. It is safe to assume, however, that in the export trade with southern China, Great Britain has a commanding lead, with Ger-many second. The representatives of the manufacturers of these countries are in close, keen competition, and not infrequently the Brit-ish house is worsted because of its conservatism and disinclination to indulge in the methods employed by the Germans to secure govern-ment or private contracts. France and other European countries and Japan are also competitors, but as compared with Great Britain and Germany their showing is unimportant.

Hongkong supplies Canton and points beyond on the West River, Swatow, Amoy, Fuchau, and Formosa, with practically all the goods imported for native consumption. The country tributary to the

Hongkong market is of vast area, and no accurate estimate of its population has ever been made, but it is sufficiently large to present an attractive field for American invasion with commodities which are not now represented to any appreciable extent in southern China. With Great Britain so firmly intrenched and with the competition so keen that a small margin of profit is the rule rather than the exception, the introduction of other American goods might be regarded as an undertaking requiring larger investments, with smaller and slower returns, than the conditions would appear to warrant. This is unquestionably true from the view point of the American manufacturer, whose business education has been along the lines of quick returns on capital invested, but in the export trade with China these views must undergo a radical change in order to insure ultimate success.

PATIENCE DEMANDED.

The building up of a paying business in southern China is and always has been a slow, tedious process, in which the first two or three years not infrequently show a loss, and unless the American manufacturer is prepared to meet such a contingency without abandoning the field, it will be practically useless for him to enter the competition. British and German firms have repeatedly demonstrated the necessity and value of untiring effort, persistency, and patience under money losses, that they might permanently establish their particular lines, and American goods, of whatever description, not now in the market, can not be introduced without the expenditure of money on which no immediate returns may be expected. As an offset for this somewhat discouraging outlook for the opening up of new lines in the export trade of southern China may be mentioned the steadily increasing demand for " chops " which have been firmly established in the market and whose standard has invariably been maintained. When the native merchants are satisfied with the quality and price of a certain line of goods and their sales demonstrate the soundness of their judgment, the goods will sell themselves and a market of constantly increasing proportions is opened.

American commercial enterprises have been established in Hongkong and ports in southern China, but according to those who are familiar with the situation great difficulty was experienced in introducing their goods, sales were infrequent, losses were sustained, and finally, with patience exhausted, the attempt was abandoned. No greater mistake could have been made, taking into consideration the peculiarities of the natives and the time necessary to establish a market, for if the goods could be laid down at a price that would enable the American dealer to enter the field, and if the quality of his wares was as good or superior to those already on the market, it was only a question of time when their merit would be recognized and the business started on a successful career. There are no keener traders than the Chinese, but they are slow to act, and it is difficult to gain their confidence. When, however, satisfactory business relations are established between the importer and the native merchant, and no mistakes are made in exporting cargoes of a quality inferior to the sample or to that previously disposed of, no further difficulties need be apprehended.

FOREIGNERS HANDLE AMERICAN GOODS.

With the possible exception of flour, kerosene oil, sewing machines, cigarettes and tobacco, and canned goods, no American goods imported into Hongkong are represented by Americans. This condition is a serious handicap in the effort to establish and maintain trade in other commodities exported from the United States. While the British and German houses handle American goods, and express a willingness and even a desire further to extend their connections in this direction, it is inevitable that they should give the preference to the same class of commodities exported from their own countries if, by so doing, they incur no business loss. British and German houses establish themselves, and with the aid of young men sent out from home to be trained in the business, gradually erect an imposing structure of commercial enterprise. These young men begin at the bottom on modest salaries, usually learn the Chinese language, and are advanced to places of trust as their usefulness develops. One of these young men eventually becomes the manager of a vast business, for with the British and German firms no " son of his father " or relative of the president of the manufacturing company whose goods they handle can be appointed to a sinecure. They are out there for business and they get it by application, a close study of the market, importing goods, whatever they may be, that the whims and caprices of the Chinese demand, and by establishing a reputation for stability and reliability. If their methods were emulated by American business houses, there is no reason why the United States should not have its share of the trade.

CANTON.

Canton is the great city of the southern part of the Empire, and its trade annually reaches enormous proportions. While it is dependent in a large degree on Hongkong for its importations because of the transshipment at that port of goods from foreign countries, it may be regarded as the chief native city in commercial importance south of Shanghai. The various guilds of Canton maintain their agents at Hongkong, where they are constantly in touch with the market and ready at all times to take advantage of favorable quotations. Under this system practically every commodity exported from Europe or America passes through the hands of the Hongkong importer before it reaches the Canton merchant, but, as in the north, it apparently gives mutual satisfaction. The latest official report showing the annual valuation of Canton trade is the " Returns of Trade and Trade Report " for 1904, published by the Imperial Maritime Customs. From it a fairly accurate estimate of the business transacted may be formed. The total value of Canton's trade is given at over 96,000,000 haikwan taels, which, with 1 haikwan tael as the equivalent of 66 cents gold, amounts approximately to $63,360,000. Of the total revenue collected, Great Britain paid $1,468,329, which was more than eight times the revenue trade of the other foreign nations combined. France contributed $111,540 and Germany approximately $56,000. Matting, silk, and tea are the staple exports of Canton, but because of inferior workmanship, the export of matting dropped heavily in 1904.

AMOY.

Amoy is 120 miles above Swatow and a little over 300 miles from Hongkong, between which port and Amoy two steamship lines ply regularly. Frequent calls are made at this port by ships from Europe and America, but, according to those who are familiar with the situation, there has been an alarming decadence in the trade of this district. Amoy and its surrounding territory have an emigrating population. It is estimated that eight families out of ten are at work abroad, remitting regularly to their homes a certain amount of the money earned. Such a condition is not favorable to the prosperity of a community, and the district, of which Amoy is the port and commercial center, appears to be retrograding rather than progressing. It is estimated that fully 70,000 coolies emigrate annually from Amoy to Singapore and other southern points, which must constitute a severe drain on the natural resources of the district because of the lack of men willing to develop them. The masses which remain at home are said to be satisfied with little or nothing, contenting themselves with earning enough money only to supply food and a roof to cover their heads.

It is estimated that in fifteen years the export of Chinese-grown Oolong tea from Amoy has fallen off from approximately 15,000,000 pounds to 900,000 pounds. Of this the United States imported not one pound. There were shipped, however, through the port to America in 1904 85,688 piculs or 11,324,067 pounds of Oolong tea from Formosa. The average tea crop of Formosa is estimated at 17,000,000 pounds, and the tea growers of that island are becoming convinced of the desirability of shipping direct to American ports rather than have their product transshipped at Amoy. As a result of this movement it is estimated that in the first ten months of 1905, 2,000,000 more pounds were shipped direct than in the whole of the preceding year with a crop approximately the same size. The principal importations of

American goods into Amoy, as shown by the trade returns of the Imperial Maritime Customs, are kerosene oil, tobacco and cigarettes, and flour. In piece goods and metals England controls the market, and in practically all the other commodities she has apparently a commanding lead. Germany, the Netherlands, and France appear to be her only competitors in the Amoy trade, with the exception of the American trade above noted.

FUCHAU.

Fuchau is 200 miles north of Amoy and about 420 miles south of Shanghai. It is unfortunately situated for any extended commerce. It lies several miles up the river, and ocean-going vessels, even of the lightest draft, are compelled to anchor from 12 to 15 miles from the city. Although lighterage facilities are fully adequate to meet the requirements of the shippers, the long distance from the anchorage must of necessity be a serious handicap in the prosecution of an import and export trade. Tea still forms the principal article of export from Fuchau, but this once important trade appears to be fading away, a condition only explainable by the indolence of the natives, who are becoming more and more indifferent to the necessity of planting and properly cultivating the crops. Opium is said to be primarily responsible for this condition, and, according to the tea men of Fuchau, no relief is in sight.

SWATOW.

Swatow, situated on the coast, is 190 miles north of Hongkong, on which port Swatow is dependent for all her supplies. As a result Swatow reflects the commercial conditions of Hongkong and the only American imports of any importance in 1904, according to customs returns, were flour and kerosene oil. The English control practically all other commodities brought into Swatow to be consumed there or reshipped to the interior. The construction of a railroad line from Swatow to Ch'ao-Chou-fu under Japanese supervision will, it is believed, assist materially in the development of this territory and possibly spur on the natives to renewed efforts in work for exports. As Ch'ao-Chou-fu is one of the important inland cities of China, it is reasonable to assume that the advent of railroad facilities will develop trade materially.

HANKAU.

Hankau, situated approximately 600 miles up the Yangtze River, is for more than half the year accessible to the largest ocean-going vessel. Its importance as a commercial center is growing with remarkable rapidity, and by reason of its geographical location and great natural advantages it has been appropriately named the "Chicago of

China." Nine years ago Hankau had a population of less than 200 foreigners, but its rapidly developing trade has attracted so much attention that now approximately 2,000 foreigners may be found within its limits. A circle of 10 miles would include the cities of Hankau, Wuchang, and Hanyang, with an estimated population of 2,500,000. The chief exports of Hankau are tea, hemp, and rice. In the exportation of tea this city ranks first in the Empire, and during the season it is not uncommon to see fully 30 ocean-going steamers anchored in midstream awaiting their cargoes of tea for transportation to all parts of the world. English, German, and French steamships run direct from Europe to Hankau, which, in addition to Japanese ocean going and coastwise steamers and the lines of Jardine Matterson & Co., Butterfield & Swire, and the China Merchants Navigation Company, make a total of approximately 300 vessels loading and unloading at this port. In addition to its splendid water communication, Hankau is now the southern terminus of the railroad between Peking and Hankau, and the running time under ordinary conditions is only three and one-half days. When the railroad from Hankau south to Canton, the concession for which recently passed from American to Chinese control, shall be completed, Hankau will have established her right to the claim of commercial importance second to no city in the Empire. Even now all the products of the Yangtze Valley above Hankau and those for 100 miles below center in that city for export.

One of the largest native ironworks in China is located at Hanyang, while at Wuchang are large antimony and smelter works and a Government mint. There is a factory in Hankau for the steaming, compressing into bricks, and boxing of tea for shipment all over the world, and that city is also the headquarters for the famous Hankau grass linen. Plans are now under way for the erection of a large cotton mill, presumably for the manufacture of yarn, for which there is an enormous demand throughout the Empire.

Hankau may be regarded as the geographical center of the Chinese Empire, and, with the completion of the Canton and Hankau Railroad and the development of natural resources inevitable with the establishment of rail communication through rich and populous provinces, this city, it is confidently predicted, will assume first rank among the treaty ports of China.

In 1895 the gross value of the trade of the port, foreign and native, amounted to $40,781,614, and in 1904, a period of ten years, it had increased to $97,617,074. These values are figured with 66 cents as the equivalent of 1 haikwan tael. In 1904 the imports from foreign countries were valued at $8,458,355, of which the share of the United States amounted to $183,535.

HANGCHOW.

In Hangchow and its environs it is estimated that there is a population of not less than 800,000, and while it is a city of wealth and native business enterprise, the market so far as foreign goods are concerned indicates but little evidence of attention. While the city is within a short distance of Shanghai, which ought to have some influence on the introduction of foreign products and the maintenance and development of the trade, the sale of cotton piece goods, flour, kerosene oil, machinery, and hardware is greatly restricted, and the remedy appears to be the adoption of live up-to-date American business methods. Among the articles already in use by the Chinese of Hangchow, but which are not imported to any extent from the United States, are cheap towels, cotton flannel, soap, cheap lamps, cotton umbrellas, rubber overshoes, and patent medicines. The value of this market is at present comparatively insignificant, but it could be enlarged, and our home manufacturers could participate in its development. This, however, could not be accomplished by any half-hearted measures. Competent and energetic agents, preferably with a knowledge of the Chinese language, should be sent to these backward, interior cities, where they can make a study of the needs of the market and then invade it with salable goods.

The same conditions obtain at Soochow, another city with nearly 1,000,000 inhabitants in close proximity to Shanghai, and the same remedy would apply.

CHEFOO.

Chefoo is so situated geographically as to enable it under normal conditions to supply a considerable part of the imports required by the Manchurian markets. The Chinese merchants of Niuchwang frequently visit Chefoo for the purpose of obtaining supplies of goods for distribution still farther north, and it is also the practice of the Chefoo merchants to send representatives to Niuchwang and other points to "drum up trade." The war greatly restricted the business of Chefoo; but with a return to ordinary conditions it is believed that her importance as a treaty port will again be demonstrated. It is the principal port of Shantung Province, which is under German domination. Practically the only Americans carrying on business in this city are the Standard Oil Company, L. H. Smith & Co., Zimmerman & Co., A. C. Taylor & Co., and A. C. Siemer, who has as his business associates two Chinese partners and who is developing an excellent business.

In the importations into Chefoo Japan leads, but Great Britain and Germany are satisfactorily represented. With the exception of piece goods, kerosene oil, flour, and canned goods, American products have a comparatively insignificant representation, but there is apparently no sound reason why this condition should not be improved. In laundry soaps England ships to Chefoo hundreds of cases every month. The soap is made up in 2½-pound bars, packed 20 bars to the case, and sold at retail for $5.50 Mexican a box. There is also a large demand for scented toilet soaps put up in fancy boxes. These are supplied by England and Germany, and are sold at retail for from 20 cents to 60 cents Mexican a case. Not only in Chefoo, but in other ports in China, excellent opportunities are presented for the introduction of laundry soaps. If an American should desire to enter the market, he should exercise great care in the manufacture of his soap. Complaints were frequently heard in Chefoo of the inferior quality of a German laundry soap recently introduced, which was regarded as too soft and having ingredients injurious to the articles washed.

Between 300 and 500 cases of candles are imported into Chefoo every month. They are made in England by a manufacturer named Price, and are sold at retail for 25 cents Mexican for a package containing six candles. In gray piece goods the American makes dominate the trade of Chefoo, and in 1904 there were imported 6,086,090 gallons of American oil, as against 450,000 gallons of all other oils.

BRITISH AND GERMAN METHODS.

PLANS WORTHY OF CAREFUL CONSIDERATION.

English and German shippers have adopted the plan, which is said to have accomplished good results, of sending to English or German merchants of Chefoo, as the case may be, consignments of goods of all descriptions and extending a credit to the consignee of from three to six months after their arrival. German manufacturers have gone even further, and have shipped goods for which there was no demand, with the sole idea that a market might be created by permitting the Chinese to have a "look see." Goods can be shipped direct to Chefoo, but they are usually sent to Shanghai, and from there transshipped without additional customs charges. As the duties are paid at the point of destination, the packages are not opened for examination at Shanghai. It is estimated that it requires approximately four months for goods to reach Chefoo from New York via the Suez route; but complaints are frequently heard that, through carelessness at Shanghai, consignments are held for two or three weeks before they are transshipped to Chefoo. Goods required for local consumption or for distribution are generally bought in Shanghai. Efforts are, however, now being made to enable the merchants of Chefoo to deal direct with the American and European exporters; but the success of such a movement, upsetting, as it would, long-established custom, is doubtful, except in isolated cases.

AMERICAN TRADE.

LARGE INCREASE IN COTTON MANUFACTURES.

The imports of China from the United States from 1895 to 1904 showed 413 per cent increase, as against the increase of 77.7 per cent in the imports from all countries for the same period. This is assuredly a commendable showing, and should stimulate American manufacturers to efforts, which, in addition to our natural advantages, should result in a trade expansion in the next decade that will dwarf our present commerce with China. Leaving for the present the consideration of China as a whole, the purposes of this report can be best accomplished by discussing the trade of Shanghai, which is the great distributing point for American manufactures, especially for piece goods. Figures must be taken from the returns from the Imperial Maritime Customs, and it should be explained that the statisticians connected with that service are seriously hampered in their efforts to show the country of origin by reason of the system in operation. While the accuracy of the figures can not be questioned, they are in this respect so incomplete as to be somewhat confusing. For comparison, however, an analysis so far as is practicable of the returns for 1895 and 1904 will be made, which will present the enormous proportions of this market.

COTTON PIECE GOODS.

The total value in gold, figured at 66 cents as the equivalent of 1 haikwan tael, of the imports into Shanghai from foreign countries and from Chinese ports for 1895, was $65,229,665, as against $129,957,958 in 1904. The reexports to foreign countries and Chinese ports in 1895 were valued at $49,479,237 and the reexports in 1904 at $100,067,812. Of the reexports in 1895, only $3,913,681 went to foreign countries, including Hongkong, while the value of goods reexported to Chinese ports amounted to $45,565,555. In 1904 the reexports to foreign countries were valued at $5,945,683, and the reexports to Chinese ports amounted to $94,122,128.

In 1895 the total imports into China amounted to $134,610,000, of which Shanghai received $65,230,000 in round numbers, or 48.5 per cent. In 1904 the imports were $240,154,000, and Shanghai's share was $129,958,000, or 54.1 per cent. This shows an increase of only 5.6 per cent in the total importation into Shanghai for the last decade, for the reason that there were decreased importations in certain commodities, others remained practically the same, while several indicated a gratifying increase. Among the latter, American piece goods were conspicuous, as they formed the great bulk of our exports to China through Shanghai.

COMPETING COUNTRIES COMPARED.

As Great Britain, the United States, the Netherlands, and Japan were the largest importers of gray piece goods in 1895 and 1904, these four countries have been selected for comparison, and in the accompanying tables the quantities and values of shirtings, drills, jeans, and sheetings imported are shown under the classifications as they appear in the reports of the Imperial Maritime Customs. The figures show that the importations from the United States have increased from 1,497,756 pieces, valued at $3,106,000, in 1895 to 3,774,675 pieces, valued at $8,596,972, in 1904. The importations from Great Britain were smaller by 1,836,901 pieces, valued at $1,138,415, in 1904 than in 1895. It must be remembered, however, that 66 cents, as the equivalent of 1 haikwan tael, has been used as the rate of exchange in both years. As a matter of fact, in 1895 1 haikwan tael was worth 80 cents in gold, or 14 cents more than in 1904. While this difference in exchange would affect the value of the piece goods imported from Great Britain and elsewhere, it had no bearing on the quantity. In 1904 the imports from the Netherlands were 102,732 pieces, valued at $136,576, less than in 1895, while Japan has increased her exports from 15,006 pieces, valued at $23,886, in 1895 to 157,633 pieces, valued at $277,920, in 1904.

PIECE GOODS IMPORTED INTO SHANGHAI, 1895.

Article.	Great Britain.		United States.		Netherlands.		Japan.	
	Pieces.	Value.	Pieces.	Value.	Pieces.	Value.	Pieces.	Value.
Shirtings, gray, plain	5,396,535	$8,191,940					850	$1,122
Drills	268,811	496,763	580,983	$1,317,190	84,657	$125,715	11,205	18,489
Jeans	116,760	161,829	22,000	29,040	39,030	54,096		
Sheetings	640,765	1,141,844	888,773	1,759,771	5,036	7,465	2,951	4,275
Total	6,422,871	9,992,376	1,497,756	3,106,001	128,723	187,456	15,006	23,886

PIECE GOODS IMPORTED INTO SHANGHAI, 1904.

Article.	Great Britain.		United States.		Netherlands.		Japan.	
	Pieces.	Value.	Pieces.	Value.	Pieces.	Value.	Pieces.	Value.
Shirtings, gray, plain—								
7 pounds and under	171,917	$192,891					300	$277
7 to 9 pounds	1,371,330	2,150,347	71,000	$125,116	1,200	$1,901	180	255
9 to 11 pounds	1,261,985	2,540,376	158,340	308,288	1,250	2,475	1,400	1,848
Over 11 pounds	748,096	1,811,262	18,360	40,594	300	645	2,660	5,179
Sheetings, gray, plain—								
9 to 11 pounds	2,608	5,680	678,560	1,298,764				
Over 11 pounds	565,450	1,250,210	1,361,041	3,188,919	4,500	10,247	115,380	194,185
Drills—								
Under 12¾ pounds	680	1,069	497,425	1,165,467	647	1,533	6,140	10,536
Over 12¾ pounds	108,381	221,747	842,289	2,168,052	8,116	17,945	31,573	65,640
Jeans—								
30 yards	262,044	466,927	95,660	179,936	9,978	16,134		
40 yards	93,479	212,852	52,000	121,836				
Total	4,585,970	8,853,961	3,774,675	8,596,972	25,991	50,880	157,633	277,920

It will be seen that the value of the imports of gray cotton piece goods from the United States in 1904 was 93.6 per cent of the total value of the same commodities imported from Great Britain, the Netherlands, and Japan. In 1895 the value of Shanghai's imports of gray goods from the United States amounted to only 14.7 per cent of the combined valuation of similar exports from Great Britain, the Netherlands, and Japan. These figures indicate a most satisfactory growth in the popularity of American gray piece goods.

REEXPORTS FROM SHANGHAI.

In 1895 the total number of pieces of this same class of goods reexported from Shanghai to Chinese ports was 6,560,915, valued at $10,872,412, of which only $3,028,461, or 27.9 per cent, was credited to the United States. In 1904 the total reexports amounted to 8,391,292 pieces, valued at $17,750,751, and the value of the American gray goods reexported that year from Shanghai was estimated by the Imperial Maritime Customs returns at $9,256,751, or 52.2 per cent, of the total valuation. The total imports of Shanghai in 1904 were valued at $114,689,417. These figures are exclusive of opium, which amounted to $14,027,701. In the same year there were imported into Shanghai cotton goods valued at $29,585,164, which formed 25.7 per cent of the total importation. Of this $29,585,164, including the value of cotton yarns extensively imported into Shanghai, our share under normal conditions should be materially increased. An examination of the list of piece goods extensively in use in central and northern China shows that the English dominate the trade, as is forcibly shown in the reexports from Shanghai to the northern markets. It seems highly improbable that we can not manufacture these goods and lay them down in the ports of China at prices which will enable them to compete with similar articles of European make.

SUPERIORITY OF AMERICAN COTTONS.

American gray cotton piece goods control the markets of northern China, not only because of superiority in quality and greater adaptability to the climatic conditions, but for the reason that the Chinese now fully appreciate that they practice real economy in buying pure, unsized cotton goods manufactured without the use of any foreign matter. It is through the realization by the natives of the north that heavily-sized piece goods, weight for weight, are inferior in every respect to the pure article, that the importations of English makes have steadily decreased, while succeeding years show more than a proportionate increase in the demand for American goods. The goods sold themselves after they were properly introduced and firmly established in the market through the untiring efforts and business-like methods of the dealers in American piece goods in Shanghai and the surrounding territory. It has taken many years to build up this splendid trade, and its maintenance and expansion now rest to a far greater extent with the American manufacturer than with the merchants of northern China who handle the goods. It is undeniable that there has been gross negligence on the part of some American shippers in exporting to China. While the consistent and even rapid growth of trade in American manufactures in central and northern China affords ample proof that our fabrics are steadily gaining appreciation throughout that country, there are certain obstacles hampering expansion.

RULES FOR EXPORTERS.

Careful attention to these points is absolutely essential if American manufacturers desire to participate in the vastly increased demand inevitable with the close of the war and the opening up of Manchuria:

(1) The indifference of manufacturers to the necessity of rigidly maintaining and improving the quality of their output when it has obtained a standing and ready sale on the market.

(2) Their lack of due adherence to the terms of contracts entered into as to the time of delivery. This is of grave importance, inasmuch as upon prompt delivery according to stipulations depends the proper fulfillment of contracts made with native merchants.

(3) The insecure and inefficient packing of piece goods cargoes frequently complained of on their arrival in China. Through such carelessness damage often results, entailing not only serious loss but great annoyance to the merchants because of their inability to make delivery of contracts to their Chinese customers. It must be borne in mind that goods are subjected on the railroads and steamships to excedingly rough handling, needlessly so, possibly, but nevertheless calculated to destroy, partially at least, any packing of insufficient strength to withstand it. Goods destined for the Orient require the best protection that can be afforded, and the difference in expense is so slight that the methods now frequently employed must be due rather to carelessness than to a consideration of the fractionally greater cost.

(4) The delay in transshipping on the Pacific coast, through which goods required in China at the earliest possible moment to fill contracts with the native merchants, are held for long periods. According to foreign merchants in Shanghai and other treaty ports, this repeatedly occurred during the recent war and was the source of great annoyance and not infrequent loss.

(5) The neglect of manufacturers to maintain the weight of their goods. Every cargo of piece goods of whatever kind shipped to China should be identical in weight with the one preceding, and all should conform absolutely to the samples submitted by the importers

to the Chinese buyer. It has not infrequently happened that three pieces of goods, supposedly of the same weight and contracted for by the Chinese with that understanding, have been found to weigh 14.6, 13.6, and 14 pounds, respectively. This carelessness on the part of the shipper has led the Chinese dealer to distrust a cargo of that "chop" on all occasions, and to demand that the bales be opened so that he may have an opportunity to ascertain if the goods are up to the standard. Mistakes of that character can not successfully be explained to the Chinese, and they unquestionably constitute a menace to the trade.

(6) Manufacturers evidently fail to realize the importance of a properly-trimmed selvage. When a piece of goods is opened and the ends of the yarn are found to be sticking out, indicating careless trimming, the Chinese buyer objects, and it may, and generally does, result in a serious falling off in the demand for that particular chop.

(7) The English manufacturers have adopted a plan which it might be well for the piece-goods men of the United States to follow. At the beginning and at the end of a piece of goods they weave what is called a "heading." As the goods are sold by the importers to the Chinese buyer generally unopened, this prevents unscrupulous natives from presenting unjust claims for short lengths. No such precaution is taken by the American manufacturer.

LACK OF TRANSPORTATION FACILITIES.

Among the difficulties of merchants handling foreign goods in their efforts to extend trade is the lack of adequate transportation facilities over large sections of the country. These conditions are, however, gradually being improved through the opening up of new channels of steam traffic along the coast and in the interior. With the advent of the railroad the importers of China will be able to keep in closer touch with their markets and remove many obstacles that now operate against satisfactory business transactions with the natives of outlying provinces. The likin system of inland taxation, the lack of adequate banking facilities, and the generally unsettled state of the currency also add to their difficulties; but these, it is expected, will gradually adjust themselves, and the manufacturers of the United States should be so firmly intrenched on the market as to avail themselves immediately of the improved conditions.

STANDARD OF QUALITY.

Among the Chinese, American-made cotton goods have attained great popularity, and justly so by reason of their worth. The points of evenness of make, cleanness, and smoothness of finish are closely examined into by the native buyer, and values are assigned to the various makes accordingly. Years ago the goods were principally marketed by their chops or trade-marks, by which they became known in the distant consuming market. Certain chops met the requirements and in consequence dominated the market. Manufacturers recognizing this were careful to maintain the quality of their goods. There were then comparatively few mills in the United States catering to the foreign trade, and as the business was well established and profitable their interests lay in maintaining the standard of their several makes.

Of late years, however, the great expansion in manufacturing for export, especially throughout the Southern States of America, has resulted in throwing on the market a variety of goods under new trade-marks. Several of these, it must be admitted, were of indifferent quality with regard to the standard previously established and to which the Chinese were accustomed. The consequence has been, according to the piece-goods dealers in China, a general deterioration and less salable goods. While several of the old established chops have maintained their commanding lead, others have permitted competition to lower their standard with the consequent loss of popularity and credit. In spite of all disadvantages and shortcomings, however, the trade in American cotton goods in the last decade has developed with remarkable rapidity, in fact, far more rapidly than in English fabrics of similar description. The offtake from the Shanghai market, where virtually the entire import is centered, has grown from a total in 1895 of 1,647,000 pieces of all descriptions of American goods to a total in 1904 of 8,200,000 pieces, in round numbers. It is estimated that in 1905 fully 10,000,000 pieces of cotton goods were imported.

SHANGHAI A DISTRIBUTING POINT.

Shanghai is the distributing point for northern and central China, and a comparatively small amount of the millions of dollars' worth of goods imported annually is retained there or in the immediate neighborhood. Piece goods are brought from the United States almost exclusively, it might be said, for the northern market, and, with one or two unimportant exceptions, there is no sale for them south of the Yangtze River. A reference to the customs daily returns shows that the bulk of the American goods is reexported to Tientsin, Chefoo, and Niuchwang, from which cities (with the exception of what is required for local consumption) they find their way still farther north.

In order to be fully in touch with markets, to take advantage of exchange, and for other business reasons which make their presence desirable at the center of importation, Chinese agents are maintained in Shanghai by the various guilds of the territory which draws its supplies from Shanghai. The piece-goods guild, as an illustration, has its representative constantly on the ground, and when there is a demand for certain chops in his home city he is communicated with and makes his purchase from the Shanghai dealer, or what may more properly be termed the Shanghai piece-goods jobber.   There are instances where the native dealers of other cities transact their business direct, but these are infrequent and the plan can not be said to have made any great headway as yet.

SUGGESTIONS FOR MANUFACTURERS.

Drills 2.85 and 3 yards per pound are in the greatest demand and have maintained their popularity in spite of all efforts to dislodge them.   There is also a comparatively large demand for goods 3¼ yards to the pound, while a moderate market has been established for the 3½ weight.   Drills are packed in bales of 15 pieces, each piece being 40 yards long and 30 inches wide.   It is essential that the dimensions given should be followed strictly, as the goods are marketed by the piece and not by the yard.   As the bales are conveyed unopened to the interior, it can readily be seen that the slightest deviation from this rule would create a feeling of distrust and suspicion in the minds of the native dealers which it would be exceedingly difficult to eradicate. It is equally essential that the goods be of uniform weight.   These two points can not be too strongly emphasized.   The goods should be packed with a layer of stout hardware paper, covered by a substantial burlap, and roped or strapped with iron hoops, the roping preferred.

In the light-weight piece-goods market the Americans have already driven an entering wedge, and if manufacturers of the United States will supply the goods required by the Chinese and their representatives in China will push them with their accustomed vigor the breach in the solid wall of light-weight piece goods erected by the English around southern China may be so widened as to permit the entry of the advance guard of American competition and the gradual encroachment on their hitherto impregnable commercial stronghold.   The Americans with their pure unsized gray goods control the market of northern China. They should in time divide the trade of the southern market.   The Chinese of that section are now contentedly buying sized goods and sticking to the conservative idea of paying for paste instead of pure cotton.   While it is difficult to overcome Chinese prejudices, active competition would probably accomplish it.   The development of trade is, after all, largely a matter of education, and it is time that American teachers should be sent south of the Yangtze.

COMPETITION OF NATIVE FABRICS.

The constantly increasing competition of native woven fabrics made on hand looms from yarns spun in local mills or imported from India or Japan is a highly important factor in determining the ultimate outlook for the piece-goods trade.   The manufacture of these goods has assumed enormous proportions and is daily increasing. Central and northern China may be described as one huge cotton-weaving shop, especially during the winter, when the women are not required to work in the fields. Hand looms may be found in the great majority of native homes and the women devote themselves patiently, tirelessly, to the manufacture of cotton cloth. Every yard that is not required for the uses of the family is sold, and the result is that the home workers of the interior make annually through this industry an enormous amount of money from a Chinese viewpoint. This native-made cloth is coarse but strong and durable and of various measurements. Although the dimensions are smaller than those of the imported article of approximately the same quality, the goods sell for about the same price. It is impossible accurately to estimate the number of pieces exported from Shanghai annually, for the reason that the goods are all shipped by Chinese junk and do not, therefore, pass the Imperial maritime customs. They are subject only to the native likin. It is asserted, however, by those who have made a close study of the situation that from Shanghai alone there are shipped approximately 2,000,000 pieces of these goods annually. They are sent direct to Niuchwang, from which port they are distributed through Manchuria, although a large percentage of the output is consumed in Korea. By reason of their coarse weaving these goods take dye readily, which, combined with other qualities popular with the natives of northern China, apparently insures the permanency of their market. One other factor may in a measure be responsible for the great demand for these goods, and that is the budding patriotic desire on the part of the natives to patronize home industries.

FAILURE IN BLEACHED GOODS.

Strong efforts have been made by the piece-goods merchants in Shanghai to introduce American bleached goods, but so far as can be ascertained, practically every consignment sent over has been disposed of at a loss to the importer. While they were cheaper in price they were not acceptable to the Chinese because they were regarded as too narrow and were too coarsely woven. The samples of English goods to be seen at the Bureau of Manufactures might well be examined by the cotton goods men of the United States, who will find in them the kind of fabric best liked by the natives, and consequently commanding a heavy sale. If these goods could be made at home similar in every respect to the English samples there would still have to be encountered in their introduction on this market the prejudice of the natives in favor of the old established English chops. This is a difficulty that could unquestionably be surmounted, provided the price, laid down in Shanghai, compared favorably with that of the English make.

It is generally understood among the importers of China that American manufacturers as a rule are disinclined to incur the expense of fitting their mills with machinery for the purpose of experimenting with the trade of the Orient. Many fancy fabrics are a specialty of continental and English mills, but in comparison with the great branches of trade they are insignificant, and it is questionable if it would pay the American manufacturer to enter the competition in a large percentage of these fabrics exported to China. It is believed, however, that despite the unsuccessful efforts of the past an exception should be made in the case of white bleached shirtings. There is an enormous demand for them on this market. The consumption last year of these goods of European make is estimated at 2,500,000 pieces, while the importation from the United States amounts to only 1,300 pieces.

ENGLISH DESIGNERS.

Several of the more enterprising firms in England maintain one or more special designers to draw designs for printed goods, which are submitted to the Chinese merchants for their approval. Frequently designs are drawn by the natives, and, again, the English manufacturers send their own designs out for inspection. This practice is essential if the American manufacturer should desire to compete in this market in this class of goods. The fashions in fancy and dyed goods are continually changing, and it is obviously necessary to keep constantly informed of the various tastes of the consumers in order to transact business in these fabrics to advantage.

The orders for any certain design are not large, and this feature of the export trade in fancy goods would probably not appeal to the manufacturers of the United States. Reports indicate that they have declined to entertain an order for 10 or 20 cases of prints, for the reason that it was too small to command attention. In this the English manufacturers operate along entirely different lines, and undoubtedly owe much of their success in the trade with China to their careful handling of orders, large and small. They aim to obtain a foothold on the market with certain cotton goods, whatever they may be, and no order is too small for them to fill in exact accordance with instructions.

DEMAND FOR TOWELS.

Although towels are considered more of a luxury than a necessity among the natives of China, a large and steadily-growing market has been established, and the American manufacturers can obtain their share of this trade if they will make a towel that can compete in price, material, and style with those manufactured in China and Japan. In order to enter the field, however, they will be compelled to lay their product down in China at a cost that appears practically prohibitive, for the price of Chinese and Japanese toweling is extraordinarily low. The preference is for a flimsy material, closely imitating Turkish toweling, made up into small sizes. These command an enormous sale, and the market is divided between the Chinese and Japanese manufacturers. The towels made by the natives all over China are practically the same as those made by the Japanese, for the reason that the Chinese learned the industry from the Japanese and, at first, they imported from Japan the wooden machines used. A market of immense proportions for towels will eventually be established. It is already of sufficient size to invite competition, and, if the American manufacturer can export a suitable article, there appears to be no reason why a profitable and constantly increasing business can not be established.

MARKETS IN THE SOUTH.

American cotton piece goods have a discouragingly small representation in the markets of southern China, although spasmodic efforts have been made to introduce the 8¼ and 10 pound weights. In order to enter this market, with Hongkong as the distributing center, the American manufacturers must make their fabrics in exact conformity with the demand of the native buyers. For years they have been accustomed to the English piece goods, and, under the most favorable conditions, it would be difficult to dislodge them, but merchants who thoroughly understand the situation insist that the American goods could find a market with a steadily increasing demand if the manufactures would only send out marketable goods and lay them down at a price that could compete with those now finding such ready sale. The Chinese of the south demand sizing. Why not give it to them? If they are content to buy starch instead of pure goods because they prefer a finish of that kind to the rougher "feel" of the American fabric and if they demand a different weave, why not cater to their tastes? It may be put down as an incontrovertible fact that goods, however excellent their quality or satisfactory their price, can not be forced on the Chinese. It is probable that a market could be established for American piece goods which contained a less quantity of sizing than is found in the popular English fabrics, provided the finish were as smooth; but, be that as it may, if the American manufacturer desires to enter this great field with any assurance of success he must give the Chinese what they require.

SHIRTINGS AND FANCY FABRICS.

The 10-pound shirtings command a sale of approximately 10,000 bales a year in the Hongkong market, while fully 5,000 bales of the 8¼-pound weight are disposed of annually. The 7-pound shirtings are less in demand, but at least 2,000 bales of these goods are sold every year. These shirtings are usually packed in cases which insure their arrival in good condition. The 10-pound weights are packed

50 pieces to the case, the 8¼-pound 60 pieces to the case, and the 7-pound 70 pieces to the case. Every piece of goods of whatever description shipped from England is carefully packed, and no complaints are heard that the standard of the chops is not at all times maintained. If the American manufacturer should establish a market for his fabrics in China, there should be no deviation from the rules so universally observed by his English competitor. The trade-mark should always be a guaranty of the quality of the goods.

In bleached and fancy fabrics Great Britain also controls the market, and her position appears to be unassailable. Much the same practice is pursued in Hongkong as in Shanghai with regard to the prints, and with much the same result. Designs are drawn by the representative of the Manchester mills and submitted to the Chinese merchants for approval. They are then forwarded to England, and the goods are manufactured and sent out at the earliest possible moment. Styles may change, but the English or Chinese designer is always so closely in touch with the situation that the new patterns are in the market in ample time to supply the demand. The market for jeans, T-cloths, chintzes, and Italians is also so strongly dominated by the English that competing manufacturers of other countries would find it a difficult task to obtain a foothold.

The efforts of the Japanese to introduce their piece goods in southern China demand serious attention. With their cheap labor and low freight rates they are enabled to sell 14-pound cotton goods, measuring 36 inches by 40 yards, 40 cents per piece lower than their competitors. It is declared by the Chinese that the manufacturers of Japan are producing an excellent quality, which compares favorably with the piece goods now popular in the market, and that if they can make other weights at correspondingly low prices they will eventually be able to take a commanding position in the piece-goods trade. The native Chinese are also manufacturing, in immense quantities, cloth for wearing apparel from yarn imported from India.

DEMAND FOR YARN.

The phenomenal increase in recent years in the demand in China for cotton yarn has created a special interest in that commodity, and the great manufacturing countries, with the United States as the single exception, have recognized the great importance of the trade and have made every effort to benefit by its expansion. It can not be stated too frequently or too emphatically that American manufacturers should make a careful investigation of this market. The importation of cotton yarn into Shanghai for distribution in central and northern China has made rapid progress since 1892, when it first attracted statistical notice. It is reasonable to assume that its growth will continue steadily to develop, because of the steadily increasing demand among the poorer classes for the yarn from which they manufacture their wearing apparel. There are now represented in the market Indian, Japanese, English, and Chinese yarns, but apparently no systematic effort has ever been made to introduce cotton yarn of American manufacture. This lack of representation in a market where the demand has been constantly increasing during the last fifteen years may be ascribed as much probably to the absence of explicit information regarding conditions and the possibility for the introduction of American yarns as to the impression that it would be difficult to lay down the product at a price that would enable our manufacturers to compete with India, Japan, and England and still make a margin of profit that would justify them in entering the field. The Indian yarn imported for this market is manufactured largely from Indian cotton, although when mixed with American cotton it produces a yarn better liked by the Chinese consumer, because of its greater strength. The Japanese yarn is usually made of a mixture of Indian and Chinese cotton, although of late American cotton has been used and, as in the Indian yarn, produces a far better article. English yarn is manufactured largely from cotton imported from the United States, made into yarn in English mills, and laid down in China at a price which enables it to compete with the Indian, Japanese, and Chinese manufacturers.

Inasmuch as the Indian mills have been making a profit of at least $5.50 gold a bale on yarn exported to China over and above the expense of manufacture, freight rates, insurance, and wharf charges, it is fair to assume that the American manufacturer can enter the market, although at a much smaller margin of profit because of the greater freight rates. If yarn from the United States can be introduced at a price permitting of a small though safe margin for the manufacturer, but sufficiently low to compete with India and Japan, a great industry may be built up. The experiment has never been tried and possibly the beginning should be made in a small way. Suppose the manufacturer satisfied himself that he could lay down his goods in China as cheaply as can the Indian manufacturer, would it not be worth while to ship to a responsible dealer a small consignment, for instance, of 16s and 20s? It would certainly be to this dealer's interest to push the American yarn to the utmost with a view to creating a market and establishing a permanent and paying connection.

TRADE OPPORTUNITIES.

FIELD FOR AMERICAN MANUFACTURES.

Flour is one of the most important exports from the United States to China.

In 1904 practically every pound of flour imported into China came from the United States, but the boycott started a movement by which the Australian product has been introduced, and vigorous efforts are now being made to increase the demand for it and maintain the supply. A commercial agent, under the direction of the Australian Government, visited China last year for the purpose of investigating trade conditions and reported that, although the United States controlled the market, there was an opening for Australian flour, which, if properly worked, could be developed into a paying business. It is known that wheat can be grown in Manchuria comparing favorably with the best quality raised in the United States, and this, it is maintained, will lead to the erection and operation of mills which will be able to supply a good grade of flour at prices below those at which the American flour can be sold. The grinding of Manchurian wheat into flour by mills owned wholly or in part by the Chinese is merely a question of opportunity and capital, and eventually the flour made in Chinese mills of Chinese wheat will control the market of northern China.

NATIVE FLOUR MILLS.

In Shanghai alone there are six companies operating flour mills, and as two of the companies own double mills there are in reality eight in active operation. The erection of a ninth mill has just been completed, and the machinery, which is in part American and part English, has been installed. The estimated output of this mill will be 700 barrels a day. Of these eight mills all are owned by the Chinese excepting the China flour mill, which is controlled by both foreign and native capital. In every instance, however, the mills are operated under foreign supervision. The combined output of the eight mills is 3,000 barrels a day, and of this quantity approximately 1,800 barrels a day are turned out by the mills using American machinery. Chinese labor is employed exclusively. The flour manufactured is not of high grade. Although it has a white appearance and looks strong, the wheat is comparatively free from gluten and the result is a weak product.

The United States exported enormous quantities of flour to Hongkong for distribution throughout China, but the boycott was so severe in that section that the business was practically ruined. It is feared that it will take months if not years to rebuild this splendid trade, which was established and developed through the earnest, conscientious efforts of the representatives there of American flour mills.

ELECTRICAL AND OTHER MACHINERY.

The opportunities in China for the introduction of electrical machinery and supplies seem to have been practically overlooked, and the vast field is certainly worthy of careful investigation. China has enjoyed less development along civil and electrical engineering lines than any other country of its size and importance. The field has evidently appealed to German, British, and Japanese firms, for they are on the ground, although poorly equippe ! to han :le the business which has offered and will continue to present great opportunities for our home engineers and manufacturers if they will employ the same energy and business ability that characterize their operations and assure success in the Unite:l States.   Shanghai has un:ler municipal control unquestionably the best equippe i electrical plant in China, and a franchise has recently been grante l for a mo ern electric-railway system; Canton has also an electric light and power company, which has a thirty-year monopoly; Hongkong has a paying electric surface road in addition to a fair electric light and power system; Peking has an electric-light plant, and Hankau is about to acquire an electric light and power plant.   A large number of small isolated plants for both light and power are scattered throughout China, and these, acting as an introduction for larger and more elaborate work along the same lines, are gradually being supplanted by general plants.   It may be assumed that these central plants will, in turn, educate and prepare the native population for the great construction work which unquestionably offers opportunities for American skill and enterprise.

AUTOMOBILES.

China presents a steadily increasing market for automobiles, and the sale of machines of American make has kept pace with the demand. While the purchase of cars to this time has been confined almost exclusively to the foreigners, the wealthier Chinese now regard this mode of travel with especial favor, and as they are well able to afford the luxury it is safe to assume that the demand will soon extend to them.   Chinese drivers of automobiles are the rule rather than the exception, and this familiarity with the running of the machine, its speed, comfort, and utility, is assisting materially in influencing the natives in its favor.   While American machines are firmly established on the market and have repeatedly demonstrated their superiority over cars ma.le in other countries, it would be well for the manufacturers of the United States carefully to observe the suggestions which are regarded as essential to the increase of the sale of American automobiles.   They should give prompt attention to filling and shipping orders.   Close attention should be paid to the details of the shipment.   No car should leave the United States unless its equipment is complete.   Freight rates on automobiles are high, both by San Francisco and the Suez Canal, and while it may be difficult to procure any reduction because of the comparatively limited number exported to the Orient, it is suggested that some action be taken, in the interest of the trade in the Orient, looking to cheaper transportation.

CARRIAGES AND BICYCLES.

Carriages are used extensively in Shanghai by both foreigners and natives.   Victorias and broughams are the most popular, both heavy vehicles, but apparently easily drawn by the hardy little Chinese ponies, which greatly outnumber the Australian horses imported for the purpose. Dealers express the belief that there is room on the Chinese market for what is known as the 2-horse trap, built with a high seat in front, accommodating two persons, and with the customary seat behind. As this would be an expensive equipage and within the financial reach of comparatively few, it is doubtful that even under the most favorable conditions more than two hundred or three hundred could be sold, and this is a liberal estimate. Dealers generally agree that a light runabout similar to those manufactured and used so extensively in the United States would command a ready sale. A vehicle of this type, according to their idea, should be lightly but substantially constructed, having the customary and necessary cut under. The wheels should be low, of uniform size, and fitted with either iron or rubber tires. The latter, although more expensive, would doubtless be preferred. It should contain one comfortable seat, covered with corduroy or some other durable and attractive material, and the lamps, which are required on all vehicles in China, should be of the smaller-sized American type.

Bicycles command a ready sale and the demand is steadily increasing. While machines manufactured in the United States are well represented and popular, the fact that English bicycles are more extensively used indicates that a more careful study of conditions should result in a far more satisfactory business for the American manufacturers. Among the Chinese, both at the treaty ports and in the interior, there is a steadily growing demand for bicycles. Their preference is for straight handle bars and spring brakes, similar to those of the Humber, manufactured in England, and for a free wheel. The Chinese are becoming more and more appreciative of the utility of the bicycle for business purposes as well as for pleasure, and if the American manufacturer would ascertain, through his representative in China, just what changes in construction would appeal most strongly to the natives it is believed that a marked increase in the demand would result.

MODERN FOOTWEAR.

An investigation of the markets of China indicates that there is an encouraging outlook for American-made shoes, although, up to the present time, the field is largely confined to foreign residents. Comparatively few natives have adopted modern footwear. It is believed, however, that the future will show a constantly increasing number of Chinamen wearing the foreign shoes, and this will open up a most attractive market. In the importation of ready-made shoes into China the United States has a commanding lead, and, according to merchants who handle these goods, this lead can be largely increased if cordial cooperation between the dealers and the manufacturers can be more firmly established. The American shoes are well known and popular among all foreign nationalities represented in the treaty ports. In order to facilitate trade, shipments conforming as nearly as possible to the styles ordered by the importer should be made promptly; the goods should be packed so that they may reach their destination in first-class condition; and large shipments should be avoided. The climate has a tendency to eat or rot the leather, causing it quickly to mildew, and for this reason dealers prefer to carry a small stock which should contain, however, as complete an assortment of the various popular styles and shapes as possible.

MARKET FOR HORSES.

For the information of those who are interested in breeding horses for shipment to foreign countries, a careful investigation was made of the markets of China and there was found to be a fair field there for the introduction of horses from the United States. That there are no American horses in China is probably due to the fact that no determined effort has ever been made to introduce them, and the market, though limited, offers inducements of which the American exporter might profitably take advantage. Practically all the horses now in use are imported from Australia, for no especial reason apparently other than that the Australians are keen traders, and with frequent consignments, in the absence of all competition, keep the market well supplied. While foreigners and the wealthy class of the Chinese are not dissatisfied with the horses now imported, it does not follow that they are so prejudiced in their favor that they would not welcome an opportunity to compare them with the American-grown animal, and horse dealers in China unhesitatingly express the belief that horses bred in the United States would not only stand the climate well, but would be only temporarily affected by the necessary change of feed.

There were 1,900 horses licensed in Shanghai in 1904, and probably 1,000 more would cover the whole number licensed in the Chinese Empire. These figures include the Chinese ponies, which greatly outnumber the Australian horses, and these two classes are the only animals used for riding and driving in China. If an American shipper should desire to enter the field in competition with the Australians, it would be necessary to arrange with a dealer to receive and handle a consignment in the way that is now customary on the market. From him such information as would be necessary for guidance in properly transporting the horses could be obtained and the commissions, incidental expenses, and terms of settlement explained. While the market is not a large one, it is of sufficient size, in the judgment of those whose opinion may be relied on, to justify a trial, with conditions favorable to the establishment of a paying industry.

BUTTER, MEATS, AND FRUITS.

That it is possible to place American butter, meats, and fresh fruits on the Chinese markets is regarded by the business men of the Empire as assured if refrigerating plants could be established on the Pacific liners. The installation of refrigerating plants in steamships plying between the Pacific coast and Shanghai for the sole purpose of exporting American meat products would hardly be justified by the conditions as disclosed by careful investigation. If, however, refrigerating plants of sufficient capacity to transport the various other perishable products of the United States were established, there is no doubt expressed among the merchants of Shanghai and northern China that a permanent market with a constantly increasing demand could be established. The success under those conditions of an effort to introduce in large quantities fresh butter made in the United States is generally conceded; the demand is surely of sufficient proportions to justify the trial if the facilities for transportation were such as invariably to insure its arrival in good condition. The Australian butter controls the market, but good judges do not hesitate to assert that a better article can be produced in the United States if the manufacturer will make the effort.

If American fruits could be laid down in China in good condition a large market could easily be established, permanently maintained, and gratifyingly increased under the characteristic American push, energy, and enterprise which are inseparable from business success at home. Oranges, lemons, and apples from the United States are now sent out in comparatively large quantities and promptly disposed of. If refrigerating plants should be established on the Pacific liners, it is suggested that the American fruit men send out an expert representative to investigate the market thoroughly and thus find a far greater outlet for their products.

THE JINRIKISHA AND WHEELBARROW.

The jinrikisha, drawn by a human being, is an institution of China. This two-wheeled, smooth-running, and comparatively comfortable vehicle, in which a passenger may ride at a reasonable fare, is deservedly popular, not alone among the Chinese, but with the foreigners, who find the jinrikisha of great utility for short distances during business hours. The jinrikishas are found in greater or less numbers throughout the Empire, while thousands are in use in large cities, indicating the enormous and constantly increasing demand for them. The large annual transactions may be more fully understood when it is realized that their life scarcely ever extends beyond three years, and that even the best of their parts are practically useless in the construction of new jinrikishas.

It might be profitable for the American steel men to send an expert to China to investigate the possibility of introducing steel into the construction of the jinrikisha. From all appearances and through inquiry among the jinrikisha masters the plan looks feasible. The principle, roughly speaking, might be the same as that of the American contract wheelbarrow, with reenforcements and economy of material effected in much the same manner as in the barrow. As a suggestion (made by a member of a jinrikisha syndicate) the two sides and back might be stamped out of steel. The steel should be as thin as possible, but of sufficient strength to withstand the rough usage to which the jinrikishas are subjected by the coolies. At the same time the ornamentations, consisting of corrugations, flutings, or whatever might be deemed advisable, could be stamped. Angle steel or tubing could be used for reenforcement, whichever might be the easier made and the stronger, to insure durability. The hood hoops are now made of bamboo, and it is suggested that thin steel might be substituted, as the covering could be quite as easily attached. The floor, it is assumed, could be made of steel and possibly covered with wood for the greater comfort of the passengers. The pulling bars or shafts, it is quite possible, will still have to be made of wood, because of the lack of flexibility and the preference of the jinrikisha coolie, although this is a minor detail.

It is also suggested that should the steel-constructed jinrikisha appeal to the American expert as feasible, the vehicle be made to imitate as closely as possible the Japanese jinrikisha in style, finish, and weight, eliminating, of course, the Japanese plan of a flimsily built article.

Another institution of China is the wooden wheelbarrow to which the natives are so firmly attached that it is problematical whether any change from this cumbersome vehicle would be acceptable. An investigation was made, however, with a view to placing a description of the vehicle before the American manufacturers and inviting their attention to the practically limitless market.

SEWING MACHINES.

The United States controls practically the entire sewing machine market in China. The bulk of the trade is in the hands of the Singer Sewing Machine Company, but the "New Home" "Domestic," and "Standard" sewing machines, all of American manufacture, are also represented in the market through commission houses. Their sales are, however, limited, which may be attributed more to a lack of effort properly to introduce them than to inferiority to other makes in style, finish, durability or work turned out.

In central and northern China a few German sewing machines are imported through commission houses, but although their prices are from 30 to 50 per cent lower than those of the American machine, customs returns indicate that their sales constitute not over one-tenth of the business transacted. A determined effort has recently been made to introduce machines of Japanese manufacture but with poor success.

An effort is to be made in the near future to dispose of sewing machines to the Chinese Government. Under edicts recently issued the military have adopted a uniform half foreign and half native, and it is believed that still further concessions to comfort and utility will be made which will cause the army gradually to accustom itself to the foreign style of dress in its entirety. In order economically and expeditiously to manufacture these proposed new uniforms, representatives of the American companies believe that sewing machines will be introduced and that their work will be so satisfactory that large orders will result.

TINNED GOODS.

The consumption of canned fruits in China is confined almost exclusively to the foreigners, although within the last year a slight demand has been noticeable among the wealthier class of natives. The trade even though it be so restricted, is well worthy of cultivation, and its development in the Chinese markets is receiving careful attention. Fully 60 per cent of the trade in canned fruits is confined to the brand known as seconds. The fruit which is packed in a light sirup is of an inferior grade, but sound and palatable. The standards, with larger and more carefully selected fruit of better color and put up in a heavier sirup, command a sale of approximately 25 per cent of the entire importation. Still larger and better selected fruit with 20 degrees sirup are used for the extra standard grade. The sale of these goods is about 10 per cent of the total. The extras made from the finest fruit obtainable, as to size and color, and containing between 30 and 40 degrees of sirup, command a sale of approximately 5 per cent of the canned fruits on the market. The fruits raised in China are practically without flavor, and as they are unsatisfactory for canning purposes, that industry has never flourished in the Empire.

BRITISH DOMINATION.

Notwithstanding the rebate on tin, its cost, combined with the cost of sugar, renders it impossible for our home manufacturers to compete with the great English exporters whose jams control the markets of the Orient. The prices of their products, laid down in China, are so low as to defy American competition, and this appears to eliminate us as a factor in that especially inviting market. It is an open trade secret that there is shipped annually from San Francisco to England large quantities of fruit pulp (the lowest grade of fruit which is used for pies, etc.). It is there made into jams and shipped to the Far East to help strengthen the commercial barrier erected against similar goods of American make. It is evident that in this as in cotton piece goods we supply England with the raw material from which she manufactures and exports to the Orient goods with which we can not compete in price.

UNITED STATES LEADS IN VEGETABLES.

A comparatively small market for canned vegetables has been established in China, and in this, as in canned fruits, the foreigners are the chief consumers. The products of the United States have practically no competition, with the exception of small peas, in which France has been making a strong bid for supremacy. California now controls the canned asparagus trade, which formerly belonged to France and Germany. Aside from the excellence of this California vegetable, there is an unanswerable argument in its favor. California asparagus can be sold in the markets of the Orient 35 per cent under the European prices.

With the exception of canned meats for army and navy use, there is a discouragingly small trade in those products; but, according to business men thoroughly in touch with the situation, this market is capable of development, and every effort will be made to increase the sales of the American products by those now on the ground who are handling them.

CUBE SUGAR.

American cube sugar can reach the Chinese trade, even at a higher price, because of its superiority. All cube sugar made here for export is manufactured from foreign raw sugar and refined so much better than in Hongkong that it is readily given the preference. Unfortunately, however, for this industry, the great bulk of the Chinese cube sugar trade is in 6-pound tins. The immense quantities consumed in all parts of the Empire are the product of the Hongkong refineries and put up in tins there. The American sugar men can not compete for this enormous trade for the reason that the tins can not be manufactured in the United States at a cost that will enable them to lay down in China the 6-pound tins of cube sugar demanded by the Chinese at the prevailing market quotations. This is a serious handicap and nullifies the favorable effect produced by the superior quality of our product. The goods would sell themselves if they could be landed at Shanghai at a cost that would permit of competition. The Chinese buy the German and French beet sugars during the winter months because of their lower price and because they will not melt in cold weather. The superiority of the American cube sugar is again shown by the fact that it will keep in the Tropics. The San Francisco

Western Sugar Refinery imports raw sugar from Java, refines it, and then exports to Shanghai, where it is sold in competition with the products of the Hongkong refinery. For this trade, however, it is only possible for the American company to ship in cases.

MACHINERY.

China presents a fine opportunity for the development of trade in machinery of all kinds, and it is suggested that if American manufacturers desire to secure their rightful share of the expansion, regarded as inevitable within the next few years, they should send out experts to study the requirements of the market. It is impossible to explain in detail the objections raised by the Chinese to American-made machinery; but one complaint, frequently heard and comprehensive in its scope, is that our machinery is too lightly constructed and not well adapted to the wear and tear incident to the handling by more or less inexperienced native operators. The force of this objection is generally recognized by practical men in China who have seen the abuses to which machinery is usually subjected. There is no mistaking the superiority of our milling machinery over similar goods manufactured in other countries; but while this fact is freely admitted, the heavier, stronger machinery is regarded as preferable for Chinese use. No doubt this is largely a question of education and practice, and therein lies the necessity for a practical personal representative of a manufacturing company. The services of such a man are urgently required for properly setting up the machinery. The failure to do this is not by any means uncommon in China. The advantages, too, to be derived from his helpful, practical suggestions with regard to operation and his ability and preparedness promptly to repair any damages can not be overestimated.

The demand for cotton, flour, and paper milling machinery is certain to increase rapidly, and, properly handled, there should be no doubt of the United States securing at least its proportionate share of the business. There are comparatively few sawmills in China; but this does not mean that the limit has been reached.

The possibilities of this line of machinery should be carefully investigated. The opportunity for disposing of machinery for mints has passed, at least for several years to come. The Government at Peking has awakened to the danger of a debased currency through overissue, and the authority of the provincial officials has been so curtailed as to prevent the further unlimited manufacture of copper cash pieces.

There is also a fair demand, which can unquestionably be largely increased by the application of live American business methods, for lathes, woodworking machinery, steam pumps, hand and power drilling machines, metal planers, engines and boilers, electrical machinery, dynamos and motors, valves, and fittings.

CLOTH MILLS.

The Chinese are becoming more and more impressed with the importance of establishing cotton-weaving mills for the purpose of turning out piece goods to take the place, so far as is possible, of those now imported. That there is no cotton-milling machinery manufactured in the world superior to that of American make is not questioned by experts, but the Chinese are not experts and they entertain a different opinion. Mills of this kind will, in a comparatively short time, be erected in various parts of the Empire, and it is a market that our home manufacturers can not afford to neglect. A constantly increasing demand for mining machinery for opening up the great mineral deposits of the Empire is also regarded as assured by practical business men who are closely in touch with existing conditions. These facts point clearly and unmistakably to the necessity of sending out machinery experts if our manufacturers hope to participate in the development of the trade.

PACKING OF MACHINERY.

In packing machinery for export to the Far East the greatest care should be exercised. The arrival of a machine with one or more of its parts broken is a serious mishap. The stock of the few houses dealing in American machinery is so limited that it is only on rare occasions that the broken part can be replaced in China. When this can not be done, it is necessary to send abroad for a duplicate, which, under the most favorable conditions, can not arrive in less than six weeks or two months, and it usually takes much longer. Exporters must understand that in shipping to the Orient machinery should be far more substantially packed than for the comparatively short hauls from the factory to points in the United States.

HARDWARE.

America now commands approximately 10 per cent of the importation of builders' hardware into China, but England and Germany control the trade. The great bulk of hardware used in building construction is, however, manufactured in China. In this, as in practically every other commodity exported to the Chinese Empire, American trade can be increased if our manufacturers will give careful attention to the requirements of the market. They should examine especially the sizes, shapes, finish, and general appearance of the articles preferred, should exercise the utmost care in packing, and give prompt attention to the filling of orders according to specifications.

CHEAPNESS A PRIME FACTOR.

American goods are, generally speaking, higher in price than those of other countries, and this is a decided handicap in a market where cheapness is the prime requisite. Tools made in the United States are recognized as being of superior quality and workmanship to those of England and Germany, and this has had the effect of opening up gradually a market for our wares. This, however, has been a slow tedious development, notwithstanding the efforts of the dealers in American goods, and as the demand of the Chinese has been and still is for articles of low price, no matter what may be their appearance or durability, it would seem to be a wise business move to cater to their wants. This would not necessitate the retirement of first-class goods, for which a limited and slowly growing market has been established, but it would require the introduction of cheaper tools of inferior quality modeled in accordance with the whims and prejudices of the natives.

NAILS AND GALVANIZED PIPE.

The superiority of the American cut and wire nails is recognized in China, and they command the market, at least in the central and northern parts of the Empire.

Black and galvanized pipe of American manufacture has up to last year had a limited sale because of its high price in comparison with the product of competing manufacturers. In 1905, however, the market showed a considerable expansion in the demand for American pipes and fittings, due to the determined efforts of the importers of those materials. It may be said that a breach has at last been made in the monopoly of these goods, so long and profitably enjoyed by England, and the outlook is encouraging for a still stronger invasion of the market.

In scales and balances the American products hold the market, but too little attention is paid by the American manufacturers to proper packing and the prompt filling of orders. More care in this regard would unquestionably result in increased business.

NATIVE PRODUCTIONS.

CHEAP HANDMADE ARTICLES.

Departing from a review of the imported goods on the markets of China it will be profitable to discuss cheap articles made by hand by the natives which are in universal use among the millions of the Empire. This market is practically limitless in extent, and because of its magnitude it would seem that our factories, with their improved labor-saving machinery and small cost of production, could profitably turn out these articles in such great quantities as to insure their delivery at the treaty ports at a price well within the purchasing power of the consuming masses.   If, on a careful investigation by practical experts, the feasibility of their manufacture in the United States and the subsequent establishment of a market could be satisfactorily demonstrated, it would only remain for our factories to make articles that would resemble in every particular those now in use.   It would be impossible to force an innovation on the Chinese masses, and to secure this trade it would be essential to give them exactly what they want, things to which they and their fathers and their fathers' fathers have always been accustomed.

CHINESE SHOES.

It is estimated that the common classes expend on shoes approximately $3 a year, Mexican, and the higher classes from $6 to $20 a year, Mexican.   This means an annual expenditure of several million dollars, which is now retained within the Empire.   The shoes differ but little in shape or style, and the quality of the material used in their manufacture varies only in that satin or silk or cotton is used for the uppers.   A brief description of Chinese shoes, samples of which are now in possession of the Bureau of Manufactures and available for inspection, follows:

No. 1 (man's shoe worn by Chinese merchants and shop apprentices). They have a cotton-cloth sole, cotton-cloth uppers, and cotton lining. They sell in the shops at retail for 80 cents, Mexican, a pair, or approximately 40 cents in American money.

No. 2 (coolie shoes and occasionally worn by Chinese boys in athletic sports). They have a cheap, thin leather sole, cotton-cloth uppers, and are lined with the same material, usually colored blue.   Their retail price is 50 cents Mexican a pair.

No. 3 (men's shoes worn by middle-aged and elderly Chinese gentlemen). The sole is a thin layer of leather, then a layer of paper, with the inside sole and lining of cotton cloth usually dyed blue.   The upper is of satin.   The price is $1.20 Mexican.

No. 4 (men's shoes worn by the gentry and middle-aged men of the higher class). The sole is a thin layer of leather, then a layer of paper or feathers, with an inside sole and lining of cotton usually dyed blue. The upper is made of satin.   The price is $1.40 Mexican.

No. 5 (ladies' shoes, worn by the class known as "reformed ladies," i. e., women whose feet are not bound).   The sole is a thin layer of leather, with a lining of cotton next to the foot.   The uppers are satin. They sell for 70 cents Mexican a pair, and have an enormous sale.

If these shoes are purchased in large quantities, a reduction of 10 per cent is made.   Chinese shoes are all made by hand and by probably the poorest-paid labor in the world.   The patterns are cut and given to the women, who sew the uppers together and return them to the shoemaker, who puts on the sole. They are then disposed of to the Chinese merchants, whose shops are scattered throughout the native cities.

If an American manufacturer could produce and lay these shoes down in the various ports of China at prices as low or lower than they now command, it is believed by business men that a trade of immense proportions could eventually be established. Shoes, if made here, must, however, be exact counterparts of those now made and worn in China, and any departure from this rule would instantly destroy their chances on the market. There should be no difficulty in imitating them in all essential particulars, and it would seem wise on the part of manufacturers interested in footwear to examine this proposition with the utmost care.

SCISSORS.

In the native cities may be found shop after shop selling nothing but scissors, handmade by Chinese workmen and used in enormous quantities throughout the Empire. They are of various lengths, but the most popular size is from 5 to 6 inches, including handle. The small sizes sell for approximately 60 cash, the medium size 80 cash, and the large size 210 cash. The extremely low cost of these articles, made, as they usually are, from scraps, may be better appreciated when it is explained that 1 Mexican cent is the equivalent for 9 cash.

HOUSEHOLD UTENSILS.

Spoons, cleavers, and other household utensils may also be mentioned as presenting an attractive field, because of their enormous sale. Cheap lamps are in great demand, and in these German manufacturers, after a careful survey of the market, decided that they could compete, and they now have a trade of large proportions which is constantly increasing. If experts from the United States would go into the native cities of China and make a thorough investigation of the demand for these small articles that have been overlooked by the world's traders they might discover a way for our home manufacturers to enter the field. That way once opened with a market established and developed under the methods inseparable from business success in the United States it might be that the keynote of American commercial opportunity in the Chinese Empire would be sounded.

TRADE-MARKS.

NO PROTECTION AFFORDED.

The question of trade-marks and other protection in foreign countries is one of the highest importance to manufacturers of special lines of goods. It is especially important in China, where the people are strongly wedded to custom, and where limited knowledge of progressive methods of the outside world makes them suspicious of everything that is new, regardless of any merit that may be presented. The Chinese law affords no protection to foreign trade-marks, a condition that has frequently led to serious complications. Trade-marks of goods popular on the market have been closely imitated, and a cheaper and inferior quality has been substituted and disposed of under a spurious mark. This has led to a concerted effort on the part of foreign government representatives to have the Chinese Government promulgate regulations which will minimize the abuse. Under present conditions the merchants representing foreign manufacturers file the trade-mark with their consular representative, and it is then transmitted to the custom-house, where it is recorded by number.

The only advantage accruing to the business man under this arrangement is that in the event of trade-mark regulations going into effect he may claim priority and prevent a similar mark, subsequently filed, from being used in China. This is the only object of the transaction, for the Chinese Government at present expressly disclaims any legal protection whatsoever to the foreigner against a counterfeit of his trade-mark. Should such a law go into effect, the Chinese Government could only aid a foreign merchant to the extent of preventing native dealers from selling goods masquerading under a counterfeit trade-mark. If the "chop" of a foreign manufacturer should be imitated by any other foreigner (and these instances have not been uncommon in China), his only remedy lies in prosecution through his consular representative.

TRADE CONDITIONS IN NORTHERN CHINA

By RAYMOND F. CRIST

LETTER OF SUBMITTAL.

WASHINGTON, *May 10, 1906.*

SIR: I beg to submit herewith a report on the results of the study of trade conditions in that part of the Chinese Empire assigned to me for investigation.

In pursuing this investigation it has been with two objects in mind: To obtain a general view of the existing commercial conditions, and to deal as practically as possible with specific commodities going to make up the large volume of foreign trade in northern China.

The report sets forth the results of study along these lines, giving what is believed to be the best methods whereby American manufacturers and prospective exporters may enter the markets of China, and supplying information which may be instrumental in enabling those at present engaged in this field to take advantage of the existing conditions to capture a larger share of the immense and steadily growing trade of the Far East.

Respectfully,

RAYMOND F. CRIST,
Special Agent of the Department of Commerce and Labor.

The SECRETARY OF COMMERCE AND LABOR,
Washington.

NORTHERN CHINA.

I. INTRODUCTION.

That part of the Chinese Empire comprised, roughly, between the thirty-third degree of north latitude and the southern boundary of Siberia has an area almost as great as that of the United States without Alaska, an estimated population of 200,000,000, and an average per capita purchasing of only 36 cents, as shown by the net foreign and domestic imports of $55,000,000 in 1904 of Tientsin and Niuchwang, the ports through which this territory is supplied. It is richer than fabled Cathay as a market for American manufactured goods, its millions of people having constantly increasing wants and buying power, and as a prospective source of raw materials, for its plains and valleys are fertile and intensively cultivated, its plateaus exhaustless grazing grounds, and its mountains rich in useful and precious minerals.

The territory under consideration includes an area of 2,752,000 square miles, the smaller portion of which embraces the northern part of China proper, with an area of 522,260 square miles and a population of over 134,000,000, and the larger though more sparsely populated section comprising the dependencies of East Turkestan, Sungaria, Mongolia, and Manchuria, with a combined area of 2,230,000 square miles.

INFLUENCE OF CAUCASIAN CIVILIZATION.

In considering the attitude of the Chinese toward foreigners and foreign institutions it should be borne in mind that they are intensely conservative. Their civilization antedates the Christian era, and their religion is at bottom fatalism. Such people, even though they be commercially shrewd, are slow to yield to new methods and customs, especially since the old have been found adequate for a score of centuries. Yet the past decade has witnessed a wonderful awakening and the temporary check, caused by the boycott on American goods in the southern provinces, has not been felt in northern China. Instead of an antiforeign feeling in the "open ports" there is a distinct approval of foreign wares and manners. The friendly attitude of the Peking Government, the influence of Christian missionaries, and the adoption of Western ideas in education are the chief factors in this renaissance.

STABILITY OF THE GOVERNMENT.

At no time since the trade of China has become of importance to the various nations of Europe has the integrity of the Empire been so secure as it now is. The United States and Japan have added their influence to that of other governments opposed to a division of the country, and all the nations with interests in the Far East seem convinced that the prosperity of the Empire and its people lies in allowing them the greatest freedom in solving their own problems. To this immunity from outside encroachment the Peking Government adds a constantly increasing intrinsic strength, greater now than at any time since the Boxer uprising. The native army, uniformed, armed, and drilled after the Western plan and with Japanese and Caucasians among its officers, gives evidence of high efficiency and is a great factor in maintaining internal peace. Its increasing stability and the study of Western economic ideas have given the Government the power and desire to establish a uniform currency. The new Kuping tael is to be 98.9 per cent pure silver, and when the coins are ready for circulation all customs and taxes must be paid in them and business transactions must be made in the new currency. A law against taking the new tael or subsidiary coins at less than their face value will be effective concurrently with their issue. This currency reform will ultimately wipe out the present system of provincial coinage of copper, which has flooded the Empire with large numbers of "cash." In this economic reform there is also the promise of a readjustment if not reorganization of internal taxation, which at present is burdensome to trade.

NEW EDUCATION.

Chinese youth of high caste, educated in Europe, America, and Japan, returning home have influenced the governing class. The old, almost fruitless system of schooling for the classical civil-service examinations has been discarded, and a course of study on occidental lines has been substituted. Modern educational methods and subjects have been introduced in all Government schools, and pupils from all parts of the Empire feel their influence, both in the Imperial universities and in the secondary schools.

In the Province of Pechili, Viceroy Yuan Shih-K'ai has established a system of schools beginning with the primary grades and including the universities at Tientsin and Pao-ting-fu. Ten of the larger cities have primary and secondary schools in which American, European, and Japanese teachers give instruction in arithmetic, English, geography, athletics, and military drill.   In Tientsin there are 50 primary schools of all kinds and advanced studies in language, physical science, and mechanics are pursued in the university.   Most of the supplies used in these schools are of American or European pattern made in Japan.   The classes in drawing, for instance, use oriental conceptions of the likenesses of Washington, Franklin, Lincoln, Grant, McKinley, and Roosevelt.   The equipment of the schools of mechanical engineering and electrical engineering includes the most modern machinery.   Telegraphy is taught on the latest instruments, and the wireless system is illustrated by working models.

CHINESE INITIATIVE.

The most tangible effect of the educational influences is seen in the arousing of the initiative of the upper-class Chinese.   In ever greater numbers young men are entering American and European institutions of learning, while thousands are now in Japanese schools.   The Board of Commerce in Peking is urging the chambers of commerce throughout the Empire to study international trade, and merchants are advised to extend their knowledge of affairs by travel and study abroad.

The changes outlined are extremely slow working, as Chinese conservatism honors the customs that were old when Western institutions and the Westerner himself were yet unborn.   But that a change is working in the Chinese and that they are susceptible to the influences of Western ideas, innovations, and customs is plainly shown by a glance at the articles that now go to make up the purchases from abroad.   A trip into the interior in all probability will disclose nothing of foreign make, even if the traveler look closely.   The sights most in evidence on every hand will bespeak a state of affairs unchanged for centuries.   In the personal contact with Chinese there will doubtless be seen nothing of modernism as conceived by Westerners, save with the officials and among those in the "treaty ports," and even with the latter it will be lacking.

Mass movement in a people of such immense numbers, intensely conservative and with characteristics differing from any other nation, is not to be found in individual contact and experience.   For where advancement and education pronouncedly developed is found in one individual, he finds on every hand hundreds and even thousands who are still held in the grip of past centuries.   The one is swallowed up in the masses—he seems to count as nothing in the great equation.   And yet it is just the presence of this force of education along all lines that has at last touched the senses and quickened the pulse of this vast people.

TRANSPORTATION.

RIVERS AND CANALS THE PRINCIPAL AVENUES—RAILWAYS LIMITED.

In all Asia there are only 30,000 miles of railway and in China not over 2,000 miles completed and in running order.   Transportation is largely by the numerous rivers and canals which form the medium for communication with the interior, and for regions remote from the waterways the pack train, caravan, cart, and wheelbarrow are resorted to.   In China, as elsewhere, the freight rate plays an important part in trade, and in the making of that rate the change from one form of conveyance to another and the method of transportation are the important factors.   Railway transportation is cheapest, but is extremely limited.   River rates are not high in themselves, but the transfer of freight from heavy to light draft boats makes an extra charge on goods destined to ports a few hundred miles from the coast. The last transfer from boat to pack train or caravan and the necessary splitting of freight into small bundles is another charge in the great expense.   Many interior markets will remain closed to foreign goods until better transportation facilities are provided, simply because the cumulative freight charges are more than the goods themselves are worth.

CARAVAN ROUTES.

In many parts of the country the roads are so nearly impassable that the use of carts is practically prohibited and the pack pony or camel is resorted to.   At present the great mass of the commodities transported from Tientsin and Niuchwang to the interior follow the beaten trade routes.   The northern trade or camel route passes through Peking to Kalgan, where it divides.   One branch, leading in a northwesterly direction, traverses Mongolia and passes through many large and small settlements to Urga, the principal point en route to Kiakhta, the first stop in Siberia.   From Kalgan the second or western branch leads to Kwei-hua-cheng, about 200 miles distant.   At this point it in turn divides.

The southern trade route passes through Pechili Province to Honanfu in Honan Province, thence west to Sigan in Shensi Province into Kansuh Province to Lanchow, its point of junction with the northern route.

Two other routes lead from Tientsin, one going through Peking and turning in a northeasterly direction passes through Pechili and across the eastern portion of Mongolia, entering Manchuria at Tsitsikar, a station about 300 miles northwest of Harbin.   The other follows the same general direction along the coast line of the Gulf of Pechili through Hsinmintun and Mukden into the Province of Kirin in Manchuria.   Vast quantities of foreign and native merchandise pass over all these routes annually, though less than formerly by the last-named two, due to the operation of the Chinese Imperial Railway, which follows the line of the last-described route.

INLAND NAVIGATION.

The waterways of north China are too well known to call for more than brief mention, especially as their utility is passing in those regions in which the steel rail has made its advent. In the matter of the Grand Canal, with its terminal at Tientsin, it can be said that at this point, and for several miles from the city, it is of little practical use, having the appearance of an irregularly defined body of water with walls or sides slightly above the level of the surrounding country. The Hoangho is on the average too rapid to admit of commercial navigation and would better serve as a future source of electrical power. The Liao River, on whose banks Niuchwang is situated, is an important highway, along which great quantities of native and foreign produce annually pass, and is a well-patronized route even in the presence of the railways which have been extended through that territory. The Amur and Sungari rivers during the period of their navigation—from April to September—also carry large quantities of native and foreign produce.

RAILWAYS.

The first railway in China was built in 1876 and was twice torn up by the order of the official who ruled the country about Shanghai. At present there is only 1 mile of railway to every 130,000 people. But the attitude of the governing class has changed. The mass of the people appreciated and used the railways from the first, and now the upper classes not only want new lines but, having engaged in the business themselves, are endeavoring to develop the industry instead of having the country exploited by foreign corporations. The Government has engaged in the business with profit to the people and the imperial treasury. Three distinct roads are in operation and at least a dozen concessions have been granted, on many of which construction has already begun.

With the experience gained under the native management of the Imperial Railways of North China, the Government is about to undertake a line from Peking northwest to Kalgan, a distance of about 360 li or 120 miles. The route of this road has been surveyed, and estimates place the cost of construction and equipment, with necessary rolling stock, at something over $5,000,000. The plan contemplates the completion of the road within four years after commencement and proposes drawing the necessary funds from the profits of the imperial railways to meet the expenses as the work progresses.

With the opening of the lines from Peking to Tientsin a great change was at once perceptible in the decrease of shipping from the interior by water routes. Furs, skins, hides, and straw braid, which were brought down in such quantities that at times the Peiho was congested and traffic greatly impeded at Tientsin, are now carried by rail, and the congestion in the water traffic from this cause is a thing of the past. A reduction of transportation charges from those of the slow camel and water routes has resulted from railway competition, while the shortening of the time between Tientsin and inland cities has effected a certainty of delivery which has broadened the field for the distribution of foreign commodities. The distance from Tientsin to Peking is 90 miles and from Peking to Kalgan is 120 miles, while the freight rate by rail between the former places is just one-sixth the charge for camel transportation between the latter places.

PECULIARITIES OF TRADE.

ADHERENCE TO OLD CUSTOMS AND CHOPS.

Nowhere more than in the United States do the merchants cater to the whims, fancies, and prejudices of their patrons; yet these very elements of the Chinese trade are looked upon as demands difficult and sometimes impossible to meet. The truth is that the inborn conservatism of the people of China makes them as slow to change their ideas about goods as about other things, and instead of requiring ever new styles, as Americans do, they merely demand conformity to their needs and tastes, which are limited. For many years they have confined themselves to certain trade-marks or brands in the selection of foreign commodities, and goods similarly marked or marked in some different way having proved unsatisfactory they have been led to suspect all but established "chops" or brands. It is this opposition to change that must first be reckoned with in selling to the Chinese. They are slow to buy from new sources and just as slow to desert a house with which they have opened satisfactory trade relations.

CREDIT.

The honesty of the average merchant is above question. If he can pay his debts, he will do so, because he is bound by a score of guilds and traditional ties not to default. To be sure he demands "time" in the settlement of many transactions, sometimes as long as six months or a year, but he also willingly pays interest on the outstanding obligations. Frequently large deals are consummated without the passage of a written promise to pay, and yet the losses by foreigners in Chinese trade are insignificant, so far as the failure of ultimate liquidation by native merchants is concerned.

All transactions in Tientsin foreign trade are upon the credit basis, and therefore business done on a large scale requires immense capital on the part of those engaged in foreign importations on a purely commission basis. The bulk of the foreign trade is done on commission. Payment is generally made for goods purchased in London, New York, or Hamburg by draft drawn at sixty or ninety days after sight. In no instance is payment made for a consignment until sixty days after its arrival, although it may have been delivered immediately upon its landing. After sixty days have passed interest is charged on the indebtedness to the time of settlement at rates varying from 7 to 10 per cent, regulated to the standing of the Chinese patron, and also governed somewhat by the amount of capital possessed by the foreign house. The time during which no interest is charged is included in the price at which the goods are sold and constitutes a fixed element in every transaction, together with all incidental charges.

THE COMPRADOR.

No Caucasian assumes to trade direct with the Chinese, but transacts business through the medium of an English-speaking native employee, or "comprador;" therefore a knowledge of the language is not imperative, as indeed a conversational command of all the dialects would be almost impossible. The "comprador" is an employee of the resident agent or importer, and is paid a small salary and a commission of 1 per cent on all goods sold by him. He is always a Chinese and familiar with the financial standing of the merchants with whom his principal deals. A bond is given by each comprador to the importer and he thereby becomes responsible for any loss. This makes him at once careful and independent. Frequently the salary paid him is little more than enough to pay his expenses, but the 1 per cent commission adds up so rapidly and the Chinese are so provident that many compradors have become immensely rich.

TREATY PORTS.

Foreigners, excepting representatives of foreign governments and missionaries, are allowed to live and trade only in the cities known as "open or treaty ports." There are thirty-six of these ports, most of them on the seacoast and some only partly open to trade, while in north China at present there are only four. So far as landing merchandise from foreign countries is concerned the open ports give access to most parts of the coast and navigable rivers, but the internal trade is practically closed to foreigners. The number of open ports has increased from five to thirty-six and will continue to increase, but at the present rate it will probably be many years before the interior is opened to unrestricted trade. In this, however, an exception must be made of Manchuria, where, according to an agreement recently made between the Japanese and Chinese Governments, sixteen of the larger cities are to be opened to foreign trade as soon as the evacuation of that region by Russian and Japanese troops is completed.

CUSTOMS DUTIES AND LIKIN TAXES.

The duties on practically all foreign commodities entering Chinese ports are levied upon a 5 per cent ad valorem basis. An additional tax of one-half the regular import duty is levied on goods passing to the interior under the protection of the "inland transit pass," which franks them to their destination free from further taxation. That the transit pass fails at times to afford the full measure of protection expected of it is shown by the fact that less than 60 per cent of foreign goods entering Tientsin are sent inland by this method, the remainder trusting to passing the likin tax at an expense less than the combined likin and transit levies. At Niuchwang no goods are recorded as passing inland under the transit pass system. Native imports can not be covered by the inland transit pass.

In addition to the imperial customs duties collected at ports of entry each province and sometimes a prefecture levies a tax called "likin," similar to the gate tax of cities of the Middle Ages. This likin tax must therefore be reckoned with in the internal trade of China.

BANKS AND BANKING.

There are a number of English, German, Russian, French, and Japanese banking establishments located in the foreign business sections of Tientsin and Niuchwang, while agencies for the International Banking Corporation, an American bank, are maintained in both of those places. The Yokohama Specie Bank also has a branch in the native city of Tientsin. Daily quotations of the exchange rates are received from Europe, America, and England. Drafts against documents on arriving merchandise and commercial paper are handled in much the same manner as in America. Every bank has its corps of Chinese employees, chief of whom is the comprador, who employs and pays the schroff or cashier, native bookkeepers, bank runners, market runners, and other native employees, and is custodian of the funds. In the matter of all loans to natives made by banks the comprador is invariably the guarantor and receives a commission of from one-half to 1 per cent on such transactions.

PURCHASING POWER.

The importation of merchandise by the Empire of China has been gradually increasing until it exceeds the exports by over 40 per cent. With no apparent recourse to revenue from large producing enterprises it would appear that within a short period China must cease buying abroad. A deeper view makes it possible to see that there are extensive invisible assets in the remittances from Chinese emigrants, which, together with money brought into China by foreigners and returning natives; expenditures for foreign embassies, consulates, missions, hospitals, and schools; maintenance of foreign garrisons and foreign war vessels, and expenditures of foreign moneys in the development of railways and mines, brings enough money into the Empire to more than offset the amount which goes out in paying principal and interest on loans and indemnities, thus equalizing the unfavorable balance of trade.

Another influence most cogent in its effect is the proverbial frugality of the Chinese. This factor, while probably not one that would appeal forcibly to those unfamiliar with their domestic economy, nevertheless enables them to utilize practically all their financial resources for business purposes, their daily living requirements being far below any Westerner's conception.

FUNDAMENTAL PRINCIPLES.

POINTS THAT SHOULD BE OBSERVED.

Before passing to the special phases of trade with China it will be of value to sum up the fundamental principles upon which may be built success. The Chinese carry their conservatism into foreign trade. Goods once established command ready sales if the quality is maintained, and, inversely, goods once found wanting are eschewed thereafter, although the brand may later be brought up to the standard. In short, fair dealing is appreciated in China, as in the United States, but to this requisite is added a demand on patience and for conformity to prejudices which are characteristic of the Chinese market.

The Chinese Empire should not be regarded as a dumping place for inferior goods nor as an outlet for surplus stock in times of depression at home. If it is to be of any permanent value as a market for American manufactures, it must be cultivated assiduously, sent the best grade of material of the kind in demand, and quoted the lowest prices. Although the number of people is great, their standard of living is low and the margin of existence so closely drawn that low-priced articles only can be expected to sell. Immense quantities of such articles will be taken, however, and the manufacturer may look for his profits to large sales on a moderate margin.

These points should be kept in mind:

1. The prejudices as well as the wants of the people must be considered.

2. After allowing for prejudices, goods must be of first quality consistent with low price.

3. Limitations on foreign trade and peculiarities of banking, tariff, and transportation can be met best by active resident agents of American nationality.

II. FOREIGN TRADE.

In the decade from 1894 to 1903 the net foreign imports of China grew from $124,819,000 to $209,113,000, an increase so great that in the latter year the importation of foreign goods amounted to more than the value of the entire foreign trade, both imports and exports, in 1894, which was $185,732,000. This increase was felt in all of the great divisions of the import trade. The largest percentage increase shown was in the import of yarns, which grew 161.6 per cent. Metals stood next in rank in percentage of increase, 78.9 per cent, though they were next to lowest in point of actual growth. The broad division of sundries gained 68.9 per cent, this being the largest actual increase, while piece goods made a 62.3 per cent gain. Cotton yarns show the largest actual increase in any one commodity, with piece goods taking second place.

IMPORTS INTO NORTHERN CHINA.

STEADILY INCREASING POWER TO PURCHASE.

In 1894, 16 per cent of the entire imports of the Empire went to north China. In 1903 this portion increased to 17.7 per cent, a growth which would appear to be but slight. When considered, however, in connection with the growth of the Empire's foreign importations it is seen that this territory has more than kept pace with the trade expansion. While in 1894 this portion of China took $20,832,435 worth of foreign commodities from a total of $124,819,240, in 1903 it absorbed $36,981,556, an actual increase of $16,149,121, or 77 per cent more than in 1894, while the growth of the foreign trade of the Empire during the decade was but 67.5 per cent.

That this territory has an increasing power to purchase is shown by increased sales made in most of the provinces. Partial information regarding this is obtainable from the records of the movement of goods into the interior under the inland transit pass system. Although the system does not show the disposition of more than 55 per cent of the total importations of foreign commodities into Tientsin, and shows nothing for Niuchwang, yet it is evidence of what the inhabitants of these provinces are buying and indicates commodities for which a greatly increased sale may be confidently expected. Much of the foreign goods and all of the native produce proceeds inland without the assistance of these transit passes, submitting to the "likin" levies of the native customs instead. The inland transit pass is secured by the payment of one-half of the regular import duty in addition to the usual duty upon the article, thereby entitling the goods to be passed to their destination without further taxation and delays at the native customs barriers. Native goods can not be covered by these transit passes when going inland, but another form of pass, the "outward transit pass," is issued by Government officials to protect produce bought in the interior to be brought to the coast for export. This practice prevails in the exportation of practically all of the domestic products from the port of Tientsin, although there is no similar record of the outward passage of native produce at Niuchwang.

The trade passing through Tientsin in 1905 into the several provinces aggregated $23,000,000, an increase of $8,000,000 over the preceding year, and the foreign goods sent to the interior not covered by transit passes was valued at $4,000,000, against $2,700,000 for the year 1904.

The Province of Pechili is receiving the greatest portion of the foreign goods represented in the record of the transit pass system. In 1905 the trade was valued at $13,982,424, an increase of $3,813,740 over 1904. This is quite natural, as the inhabitants of this province have long been acquainted with foreigners and their commodities. Shansi, lying directly west of and adjoining Pechili, shows an increase of $1,061,107. Undoubtedly the increase in the several provinces is due to the coming into use of a greater variety and quantity of new articles. The increased purchases made by Kirin and Fengtien (Shengking), in Manchuria, are largely due to the necessity for replenishing, from whatever source possible, the stocks depleted by the war, as the greatest supplying of the Manchurian market is done in Shanghai.

INTERNATIONAL COMPETITION.

PREFERENCE FOR EUROPEAN COMMODITIES.

The present and prospective values of the northern China market are more thoroughly appreciated by the English, Belgians, and Germans than by Americans. There is ample justification for legitimate favoring by the different nationalities of their home products. The conditions with which they are surrounded in the Chinese character as well as in the activity and willingness of their home connections to produce the things the Chinese merchant desires amply warrant such favoritism. It is evident here that England and Germany cater, in the fullest meaning of the word, to the needs, wants, and even whims, of their customers in the foreign field. Every commission broker has on hand a complete stock of samples of every variety of goods used or possible of use by the Chinese, and is in frequent receipt of all kinds of articles impossible of use by them. With this attractive and limitless array of samples to select from, the Chinese preference for English and other European commodities will be developed to the highest possible degree. The Chinese prefers to examine the article he is to buy, especially if it is some new article with the construction, management, and utility of which he is unfamiliar. He is little influenced by pictures, catalogues, and descriptive matter. From past unfortunate experiences with purchases by catalogue he can not now be prevailed upon to do business to any extent except upon demonstration, under his personal observation, of the merits and capabilities of the article to be bought.

INFLUENCE OF EUROPEAN CAPITAL.

Another potent influence in the purchase of goods and commodities of other countries, and one which strongly reacts against a broadening of the market of American products in China, is the presence of other nationalities in considerable numbers, particularly of Belgians, Germans, and English, who are constantly seeking investments for their capital in the development of the resources of the country by the building of railroads and working mines. In bringing in their locomotives and railway supplies, and mining machinery, together with the necessary equipment incident to the prosecution of their work, they attract the attention of the natives to these articles, and pave the way for the sale of others.

IMPORTERS AND SALES AGENTS.

There are very few foreign importers in Niuchwang, due to the practice of the Chinese merchants of going to Shanghai for their supplies. The Chinese merchant can go to Shanghai at a cost far below what the foreigner has to pay, and in many cases can land his goods in Niuchwang upon paying all expenses incident thereto almost as reasonably as they can be imported direct through local houses. There are but three American and European concerns here doing a general import business, one each of American, German, and English nationality. There are, however, several Japanese and Chinese engaged in importing and exporting. These foreign firms are all endeavoring to build up a direct trade, and the opportunity should be grasped by American exporters.

In other ports the sale of goods of all kinds has long been in the hands of Germans and English, regardless of the country from which commodities come. These importers, having well-established connections with their respective English or German principals, are slow to take up similar lines of American goods. They require more particular compliance with market conditions and peculiarities and greater concessions in terms [and prices from intending American exporters than will be required by importers in Niuchwang, for the simple reason that their entrance upon the market means new factors and elements that are to be reckoned with.

TEXTILES, METALS, AND SUNDRIES.

The knowledge of the need for heavy gray cottons in this part of the Chinese Empire has been of long standing, and has been taken advantage of to a great extent by American mills. The increase in consumption has been vast, and has grown more rapidly than has their exportation from America, thereby admitting other nations into the market as competitors with our mills. For many years prior to 1885 English mills dominated this market in textiles. In that year, however, the cotton exports from America, Holland, and India had grown to sufficient size to warrant mention, and in 1890 were a large factor. The sheetings, drills, and jeans produced by American mills early received the approval of the northern Chinese market, as shown by the steady demand and the preference given them over similar goods from English mills. Increasing quantities and varieties of cotton prints, dyed cloths, and velvets, as well as various kinds of woolens, also entered into the annual consumption of this market.

Besides cotton and woolen goods, of which the Chinese are buying steadily increasing quantities annually, the importations embrace copper, steel, iron, and lead and a limited variety of their manufactures.

MANCHURIAN MARKET.

OPEN DOOR TO A RICH COUNTRY.

With the opening of the new treaty ports in Manchuria and the revival of business there an immense territory, rich in agricultural and mineral resources, will again claim the attention of manufacturers of many commodities, especially agricultural implements and mining, flour, and lumber machinery. Many of the soldiers will probably remain in eastern Siberia and Manchuria, and their presence will stimulate the native population. The immense investments made by Russians, and partially developed prior to the recent war, will undoubtedly be continued, and improvements will be brought to greater perfection, while new enterprises will be initiated. In the Liaotung Peninsula, as well as in Niuchwang, Port Arthur, and Dalny, the principal commodities of American manufacture now on the market are cotton piece goods, flour, cigarettes, kerosene oil, tinned and dried fruits and vegetables, condensed milk, and confections. While there will in all likelihood be a great demand for the large commodities necessary for the development of the agricultural and mining resources of the Manchurian and Siberian regions, the extent to which the United States will participate in furnishing these materials is a question which can be answered only by the attitude the Russian commercial interests will take. Undoubtedly this region, or so much of it as is under the control of the Japanese, will shortly be thrown open to the competition of the world, but whether there will be unrestricted trade facilities in the area north of this can be answered only by the events of the future.

FOODSTUFFS.

The foodstuffs raised in north China are in many instances, especially in the garden-truck class, quite dissimilar from those with which Westerners are acquainted, and have their own Chinese names. There are, however, many fruits, such as pears and grapes which are of good quality and appearance. Walnuts of the English variety and fine large persimmons, particularly the latter, constitute a prominent dish in their season. Millet and wheat form with rice, which is largely imported, the staple. Imported flour comes almost entirely from America, while the rice is grown in southern China and the countries of southern Asia.

NEW OPEN PORTS.

In the territory under consideration there are only four treaty ports—Niuchwang, Tientsin, Chingwantao, and Chefoo—and in these only are foreigners permitted to live or to carry on trade. Even Peking is closed to foreigners as a place of residence, excepting to the representatives of foreign governments. As soon, however, as the Japanese-Chinese treaty recently made goes into effect China will throw open to international trade the following Manchurian ports: Fenghwangcheun, Liaoyang, Hsinmintun, Tielung, Tunghiangtsze, Fakumen, Tsitsihar, Khailar, Aihum, Manchuili, Changchun, Kirin, Kharbin, Ninguta, Sansing, and Hunchun.

DISTRIBUTION THROUGH TIENTSIN AND NIUCHWANG.

At present trade with the interior must be conducted entirely through the treaty ports, and the bulk of that for northern China goes through Tientsin and Niuchwang, which were thrown open to international trade by the treaty of 1860. Since that time their commercial importance has steadily grown. In 1903 Tientsin received $23,976,846 in foreign goods and Niuchwang $13,004,710, as against $16,718,315 and $4,114,123, respectively, in 1894. From this it is seen that there was a greater increase in the purchases of foreign goods through Niuchwang than Tientsin during that decade, although the total of foreign goods imported into Niuchwang in 1903 was less than that taken by Tientsin in 1894.

Almost an equal division of the imports into Tientsin and Niuchwang is made between those coming from Chinese ports and those from foreign countries and Hongkong. Shanghai is the great port of distribution, and yet a great amount of the merchandise comes to Tientsin in the bottoms originally receiving it instead of transshipping at Shanghai. Japanese, English, German, Chinese, and Norwegian ships comprise the major part of the carrying capacity for this trade. A considerable amount of reexportation of both native and foreign commodities takes place from Tientsin to Niuchwang, Chefoo, Shanghai, Vladivostok, and Siberian Russia via Kiakhta. Through this latter port from Tientsin the great bulk of the reexports of Chinese produce goes, the greatest portion of foreign goods reexported from Tientsin passing to Vladivostok. Undoubtedly many American goods destined for Siberia are included in this reexportation. The destination of the mass of imports into Tientsin and Niuchwang is the broad hinterland comprised by the territory above referred to.

TIENTSIN.

Tientsin stands second in rank among the treaty ports in the gross value of trade that passes through the port. This fact alone would be sufficient to warrant a careful investigation of her commercial resources and possibilities, but to this the more important one is to be added, that in so far as American goods are concerned Tientsin has a rival claim on Shanghai for first place. While it is true that Shanghai shows a much larger return of trade, yet it should be borne in mind that Shanghai is essentially a distributing point for the outports, which in turn pass the goods on to the interior fields. Tientsin is, therefore, the first port of China, considered as a distributing point for goods intended for direct sale to the natives. Its imports pass from the foreign importer direct to the Chinese users throughout an area of distribution larger than that which is supplied by any other port of the Empire.

The commercial growth of the city is evidenced by the fact that the gross value of trade has more than doubled since 1892. In that year it amounted to $30,000,000 in gold, and in 1899 it had increased to $68,-000,000. In 1902, after the Boxer difficulties had subsided, the value of the foreign trade rose to $72,000,000. In 1903 it was $45,000,000, and in 1904 $47,402,472. The rise and depression were due to the purchasing to replenish stocks depleted in 1900 and 1901 and the subsequent failure of extensive purchasing by the masses, whose crops and homes were destroyed in the Boxer uprising, as well as the financial stringency of 1902–3. The figures for the calendar year 1905 show that the trade advanced to a total of 100,305,098 haikwan taels. At an average of 70 cents a tael this would be $70,213,568.

Tientsin has an estimated native population of 750,000 and about 2,000 foreigners, and consists in reality of two cities, the native city and the foreign concessions. Administrative control goes with the concessions. Great Britain controls 1,000 acres, Japan 278 acres, France 230 acres, and Germany 172 acres.

NIUCHWANG.

Niuchwang is the most northerly of the Chinese treaty ports. It is situated in the Province of Shengking, Manchuria, on the Liao River, about 13 miles from the mouth, which enters the Gulf of Liaotung, the northern arm of the Gulf of Pechili. The port is ice-bound over three months a year, navigation ceasing about November 20 and being resumed the latter part of February or the early part of March. There are about 60,000 natives, 7,000 Japanese, and 200 Europeans and Americans in Niuchwang. Since the Japanese have been in control of affairs there have been many improvements in the city.

The importance of Niuchwang as a center of distribution of foreign goods is firmly established. In 1894 the gross trade of the port was $12,765,750; in the following five years it had increased to $22,770,150, and in 1903 it had further advanced to $30,665,200 Even the disturbances of the war did not materially check its trade, the year 1904 showing a total of $27,456,459, while the indications are that 1905 will be the banner year in its trade.

American piece goods, kerosene oil, flour, clocks, watches, shovels, drugs and medicines, canned meats, condensed milk, canned fruits, baking powder, breakfast foods, cocoa, chocolate, and confections are to be found in all of the general merchandise stores of Niuchwang, Port Arthur, and Dalny, and similar articles from Germany, England, Japan, and other countries. Toilet articles and soaps from France, Germany, England, Austria, and Japan are to be found in plentiful supplies. English and German hardware supplies, padlocks, nails, etc.; Austrian and German enameled wares in plates, pans, cups, buckets, basins, teakettles, lunch buckets, etc., and oil-burner stoves from Germany and America have a general sale. With the above are to be found Japanese products in great variety, all being of cheaper quality and generally imitations of popular selling articles from other countries.

STATUS OF UNITED STATES.

AMERICAN PRODUCTS REGARDED WITH FAVOR.

The United States stands alone among the great powers in having no concession in Tientsin, notwithstanding that a tract was set aside for such purpose as a result of the treaty of Peking. No actual transfer of the title ever took place, although the American consul exercised a quasi jurisdiction over the area thus designated until 1880, at which time it reverted to China, and was added to the British concession in 1902. This absence of a concession has been held by some to be of disadvantage to American commercial interests, it being urged that a concession might attract more Americans to Tientsin and through them result in increased American trade; but inasmuch as the American merchant, in carrying on business in any of the foreign concessions, has no restriction placed upon him that is not shared by all, a concession administered by American authority would confer very little advantage.

There can be no doubt, in spite of the recent boycott movement, that the Chinese people and Government, with reason, feel more kindly disposed toward Americans than toward people of other nationalities. Inquiry among natives, where the nationality of the inquirer was unknown, brought out the fact that they put American merchants upon a trifle more favorable footing than the others.

The depressing effects of the boycott on American goods waged in the southern ports of China have not been felt in the north. Instead of the prevalence of an antiforeign feeling, which would react commercially, there is a distinct approval of foreign customs and commodities. As the market prefers the goods at present turned out by American manufacturers, they should leave nothing undone that will increase this friendliness and favor, especially as manufacturers of other countries are striving for and catering to the very preferences which have been brought out by some of the American products sold in this market.

POOR SHIPPING FACILITIES.

LACK OF STEAMSHIP SERVICE RETARDS TRADE.

Principal among the obstacles to the expansion of American trade in northern China are the lack of regular and quick freight service from Atlantic ports to the Orient and the excessive rates over the transcontinental and Pacific route. Goods shipped from Liverpool or Hamburg may be relied upon to arrive within eight or nine weeks, whereas shipments from Atlantic ports of the United States not only are not made on regularly scheduled steamers, but take from three to four months to make the journey, while not infrequently six months pass between the date of placing the order and that of delivery of goods in Tientsin or Niuchwang. The German mail steamers are required to sail on schedule time, and by reason of this German merchants can rely upon the arrival of their goods within practically twenty-four hours of the time they calculate upon on receipt of cable information that they have been shipped.

American ships are seldom seen in northern China ports. This is a decided disadvantage in the sale of American commodities in this territory. Direct transportation without transshipment of German and English articles of manufacture in the ships of their own country not only insures their safe and expeditious arrival, but by reason of their regularity of arrival upon schedule time presents a factor in the commercial question upon which American manufacturers can not base their calculations. Without doubt American products are handicapped and will so continue until more and better facilities are available to enable them to have ready access to this market. The uncertainty of delivery deters foreign traders from promising goods from America for arrival at any definite time, and with the alternative product of their own country to turn to they do not hesitate to advance their home product even though it may be inferior to the American article. On the other hand, transportation facilities are such as to warrant the importer in depending with almost absolute certainty upon the arrival of European merchandise within two months.

TRANSSHIPMENT AND PACKING.

Another handicap from which United States manufacturers suffer is the additional strain upon the packing and the consequent liability to damage of the merchandise, due to the great number of transshipments to which their goods are subjected as compared with European merchandise. Under most favorable conditions a shipment of goods from Atlantic ports for Tientsin must experience at the least calculation transshipment at six different stages. In addition to the transshipments, the cargo is almost invariably landed at Shanghai instead of passing from lighter to coast steamer. This means replacing on lighters again for transfer to the ship for Tientsin.

COMMISSION AND RESIDENT AGENTS.

A SYSTEM AMERICANS HAVE OVERLOOKED.

In order to bring to the attention of the Chinese the advantages possessed by American manufactures and to overcome the disadvantage at which American products are placed by the natural inclination of Germans and English to favor goods from their home countries, there appears to be at least one desirable method which American manufacturers can adopt, and that is for them to send out goods on consignment, as do the manufacturers of other countries. This system has been urged by men engaged in the foreign trade as most desirable, and would undoubtedly result in a profitable business if conservatively carried on, but the possibilities of building up a large foreign business in any one line on the consignment basis are not very great, as the plan manifestly has its limitations, both in number of commodities and in quantity thereof that could be offered for consignment.

Engines of 20, 30, 50, or at most 75 horsepower; pumps, pressing machines, drill presses, shapers, planers, lathes, boilers, shaftings, machines for use in tanning, leather belting, leather-splitting machinery; and a general line of tool machines and other machinery if placed with reliable commission houses in Tientsin would insure their sale and result in the building up of a good export business in this field, in which there is at present a great scarcity of American machinery.

NEED OF RESIDENT AMERICAN AGENTS.

The experience of the most successful houses engaged in the foreign trade in China warrants the assertion that only through the medium of resident American representatives established in the Orient can the most successful export business be built up. If allied and noncompeting manufacturers would unite and send representatives to the ports of Shanghai, Tientsin, and Niuchwang, with headquarters at Shanghai, an immense export business to these ports would most certainly result within from three to five years. That this would prove true is amply shown in the success that has been achieved by English, German, Belgian, French, and Japanese houses engaged primarily in the importation of the products of their home countries and secondarily in handling almost all the American products sold in the Chinese market.

The impossibility of trading direct with the native merchants, the variable nature of the likin taxes, and the necessity for studying the prejudices of the buyers are in themselves sufficient arguments in favor of responsible resident agents. That these agents should be Americans will be understood from further reading of this report, as the keen international competition for the Chinese market is frequently referred to.

III. COTTON GOODS AND YARNS.

EXTENT AND VALUE OF THE NORTHERN MARKET.

In almost any section of China hand looms of ancient pattern may be seen in the houses, and their products, coarse-woven garments of cotton or wool, are worn by many people. The farther from the seacoast and more remote from foreign influences the more this homespun and woven cloth is used. Yet it is probably true that there is no large section of the Empire in which mill-made cotton goods are not known to some extent. Only the native conservatism and the high prices of transportation into the interior keep foreign-made cottons from monopolizing the whole market, for they are recognized everywhere as superior to the home product. Transportation facilities are improving, and a persistent and well-directed effort to gain a foothold in the Chinese market always succeeds in breaking through the shell of seclusion. The methods for pushing general trade may be used as well in the cotton goods and yarn trade. There is, however, this great difference: Cottons need no introduction. They are already used extensively and are in high favor. Since the market is established, the international competition for it is more keen than in other lines.

FEATURES OF SUCCESSFUL TRADE.

To meet competition American mills must be constant in their attention to the wants of their Chinese customers. It will not do to hurry goods to this market in time of depression at home and then neglect it entirely when the home market booms. Any merchant resents such treatment, and yet it seems to be the policy of some American mills. Nor will good results attend the breaking of promises to deliver goods at a certain time. No matter whose the fault, the merchant in China suffers, and he is likely to avoid further experiments. It is also a mistake to try and force a line of goods on the Chinese. Though the goods be superior in all respects to those desired by the natives, if they do not want them it is an error to force them on the market. Everything that has been said about packing in preliminary reports published in Daily and Monthly Consular and Trade Reports applies to cotton stuffs. There is no more important detail in the trade. The general statement about credits holds good also. Long-time payments are demanded, but it is safe to grant them.

SHIPPING.

In the broad sense the obstacles to quick delivery can not be removed by the exporter. Everyone in foreign trade knows, however, to what extent care in shipping goods from the factory at the earliest possible moment frequently aids delivery. Steamship companies in the oriental trade will readily furnish a schedule of sailings, and freight shipped with a definite departure in view is likely to make from three to six weeks' better time than haphazard shipments. It has been frequently stated by those in the foreign trade of Tientsin that there is a difference between f. o. b. New York prices and c. i. f. Tientsin prices of about 10 per cent to cover expenses of insurance and freight, and an additional 10 to 12 per cent to cover duty, coolie hire, interest upon sight draft to date of maturity, storage, commission of house, and commission of 1 per cent to the comprador for guaranteeing payment. From the commission house through the Chinese merchant to the retail dealer and finally to the consumer there is an additional 10 to 20 per cent, in all a difference of from 20 to 30 per cent between c. i. f. prices and retail prices.

INTERNATIONAL COMPETITION.

British manufacturers supply a large part of the demand for cotton goods notwithstanding that they buy cotton in America to be manufactured in the mills of Manchester and other English cities. India with raw cotton near her mills, Japan importing raw materials, and the Netherlands carrying much of her cotton half around the world to her mills meet the United States in this field and often discount her prices. There is not the slightest doubt that a greatly increased share of this as well as of the entire Chinese market can be won by American manufacturers and held against all competitors, nor is there doubt that that portion at present going to American houses is being striven for by our rivals, whose efforts in that direction seem to be attended with excellent results. Our strongest position is in gray goods, and for the present the sale of this commodity furnishes our greatest opportunity, although England has not ceased to bid strongly for the restoration of her lost prestige in this line. There is without doubt more expenditure of time, energy, and money annually by English manufacturers in efforts to control that part of the gray-cotton piece-goods trade which is still retained by them and in endeavoring to reclaim the ground won by America than American cotton manufacturers spend in five years looking for new markets.

UNBLEACHED CLOTHS.

The Empire's imports of gray or unbleached cloths consist of sheetings, shirtings, drills, jeans, and T-cloths, the order being that of the value of imports of each class. In 1894 they were valued at $15,381,404,

or 58 per cent of all cottons.   In this total American mills participated
to the extent of 2,006,783 pieces, valued at $4,464,047, or 28 per cent
of the total.   In the movement of cotton piece goods 40 per cent of
the entire importation went to north China through the ports of
Tientsin and Niuchwang.   While this is true of the entire imports, the
proportion of the gray goods going to these northern ports is greater
still, being 48.6 per cent, or nearly one-half of the importation of this
class of cottons.   In 1903 gray cotton goods had increased to
$21,298,532, the share for north China being maintained at over 48
per cent, or $10,398,722, of which $8,150,582 in value were supplied
by American mills, equaling 78 per cent of the total purchases of
unbleached cotton cloth by this part of China.

FIELD FOR HEAVY GOODS.

The northern portion of the Empire receives the greatest share of
American cottons, because of the climatic conditions which necessitate
heavy goods in the clothing of the people.   The severities of winter
are felt from Shantung Province north, while south of that province
the temperature becomes milder until, in the southern portion of the
Empire, there is an entire absence of cold weather at any time of the
year, thus doing away with the necessity for heavy, substantial cotton
sheetings, drills, and jeans and the heavier shirtings which are supplied in such large quantities by American mills.   In their stead the
light, flimsy sized white cottons, prints, and dyed stuffs are required,
and they come in the most part from English mills.

GRAY SHEETINGS.

Gray sheetings are used to a greater extent than any other one class
of cotton cloth by the masses of the population throughout the entire
northern portion of the Empire in making their coats, trousers, linings
for garments, underclothing, bedclothing, etc.   The areas supplied
from Tientsin with gray sheetings are set forth in the following table,
representing the number of pieces distributed in 1904:

Province.	American.	English.	Japanese.
Pechili	529,828	8,991	60
Shansi	242,462	18,342	665
Shantung	8,665	6,255	26
Honan	9,267	1,376	
Kansuh	11,291	4,280	
Shensi	159	86	
Fengtien	23,501	229	
Turkestan	1,079	6	
Kirin	8,004	10	

The importation of gray sheetings in 1904 into Tientsin amounted
to 798,482 pieces, at a valuation of $2,178,630, and into Niuchwang
1,148,884 pieces, at a valuation of $2,619,755.   As the distribution
noted from Tientsin exceeds the importation, it is evident that there
were included many pieces from old stocks.

The total receipts at Tientsin in 1905 from the United States, England, and Japan were 2,474,148 pieces, valued at $5,622,270. The amounts sold by each of those countries in this port is next shown:

Country.	1904.		1905.	
	Pieces.	Value.	Pieces.	Value.
United States	664,401	$1,812,482	2,171,563	$4,985,664
Japan	66,160	184,747	208,856	424,657
England	56,986	150,729	93,729	211,949
Others	10,935	30,672	70,456	145,730
Total	798,482	2,178,630	2,544,604	5,768,000

A comparison of the two years shows the remarkable increase in the purchase of gray sheetings to be due almost entirely to the phenomenal demand for the American article. During the first nine months of 1905 the amount of American goods delivered exceeded the total importation of gray sheetings during the year 1904. In fact, they exceeded the total value of these goods imported from all countries in any year since 1899, save that of 1902, while the purchases for the entire year are the greatest in the history of the port of Tientsin. The ratio of increase in Japanese goods is about the same as shown by American sheetings. Although the total is small, it is significant of the future when we view the great activity of Japanese cotton manufacturers, the rapid improvement in the quality of their goods, and the natural geographical advantages possessed by them over all other competitors. That Japan has come into this market and in the short space of ten years displaced such a strong competitor as England speaks volumes. The showing made by the English, while indicating an increased sale for the whole of this year, does not present a very flattering picture.

Gray sheetings are shipped in trusses of two bales, each bale containing 20 pieces. The bales are bound together in the formation of the truss by 8 or 9 turns of rope of ⅝-inch diameter and 4 or 6 iron straps, the whole being machine pressed. In many instances either the rope is entirely or partially gone and frequently all of the iron straps save one have become broken in transit.

GRAY SHIRTINGS.

Gray shirtings are used in making garments by city and country natives. In all cases they are dyed before being made into clothing, the dyeing being done in small establishments or the home. Indigo blue and pale blues and grays are the most popular.

The distribution of American gray shirtings from Tientsin is limited to four provinces, including Pechili, which consumed 1,799 pieces in 1904. The adjoining Province of Honan was the next largest user, taking 1,561 pieces. In fact, to these two provinces the bulk of the goods were sent, Shansi and Kansuh receiving the remainder, 192 pieces and 6 pieces, respectively.

In 1904 northern China took 121,331 pieces of American gray shirtings, valued at $239,533, as against 568,586 pieces of English gray shirtings, valued at $872,302. In these shirtings the greatest showing made by the American product was in the heavier weights. The quantities and values of American, English, and Japanese gray shirtings imported in 1904 are given below:

Weight.	American.		English.		Japanese.	
	Pieces.	Value.	Pieces.	Value.	Pieces.	Value.
7 pounds and under.....................	3,800	$4,013	63,145	$66,168	1,500	$1,683
Over 7 pounds and not over 9 pounds ..	13,722	19,987	330,052	460,725	....	....
Over 9 pounds and not over 11 pounds .	45,040	86,584	117,603	216,874	....	....
Over 11 pounds	58,794	96,961	57,730	127,533	200	429

The last item seems to indicate that Japanese mills are beginning to supply some of the heavier weights of gray shirtings. It further appears that in Tientsin during 1905 the Japanese sold 2,640 pieces of gray shirtings of similar weights, the total imports aggregating 798,085 pieces, the United States and England participating as follows:

Weight.	United States.		England.	
	Pieces.	Value.	Pieces.	Value.
7 pounds and under ......:	....	....	97,644	$109,361
Over 7 pounds and not over 9 pounds........................	16,550	$27,804	481,469	27,804
Over 9 pounds and not over 11 pounds.......................	34,210	65,854	123,184	250,032
Over 11 pounds................................	9,460	22,514	16,128	38,384

Gray shirtings range from 6-pound pieces to 13-pound pieces. The prevailing widths are 38 to 39 inches in 38 to 39 yard lengths, although 40-yard lengths are manufactured in 36-inch widths.

AMERICAN DRILLS.

In gray drills the product from America leads all others. The total value of drills does not equal that of gray sheetings or shirtings, but exceeds that of white shirtings. The quantity sold by American mills in north China in 1904 was 666,500 pieces as against 164,039 by the English, Dutch, Indian, and Japanese competitors. The following statement shows the remarkable increase of American drills, and the value of the sales of other countries at Tientsin:.

Country.	1905.		1904.	
	Pieces.	Value.	Pieces.	Value.
United States	745,628	$1,870,017	224,240	$532,252
Japan...................................	51,176	112,543	94,961	244,236
England...................................	76,581	175,543	31,483	77,611
Netherlands...................................	21,515	48,764	3,040	7,041
India.......................................	28,747	70,186	21,065	50,241
Total.................................	203,647	2,277,053	374,789	911,381

The quality of the American product is always spoken of in the highest terms by the importers; its superiority over other products is claimed by all. The reduction in the sale of Japanese drills appears to be due to two causes—the supply of the army needs and, latterly, stocking the Manchurian market. The duty on drills is $7\frac{3}{4}$ cents per piece weighing $12\frac{3}{4}$ pounds and under, and 9.7 cents for weights over $12\frac{3}{4}$ pounds for pieces not exceeding 31 inches in width and 40 yards in length. Drills are used to a larger extent by country folk than by residents of cities. They are made up into clothing for spring, fall, and winter wear in such articles as jackets, coats, vests, and over garments. They are locally dyed in blues and grays. American drills received at Tientsin are sold in varying quantities throughout the nine Provinces of Pechili, Shansi, Shantung, Honan, Kansuh, Shensi, Fengtien, Turkestan, and Kirin.

JEANS.

Jeans may be placed among the less important gray cloths imported through Tientsin and Niuchwang. The American product, however, forms the greatest portion of the importations received from any one country, the more important port with respect to this class of cloth being Niuchwang. Jeans have been much in use by residents of both cities and the country, but its use, as well as T-cloths, is being displaced by cotton Italians. It is still in favor in certain localities with residents in country places and appears to be growing somewhat in popularity in the region supplied more particularly by Niuchwang. It enters into the making of the various articles of clothing and is dyed locally by the natives.

T-CLOTHS.

This class of goods does not appear to have greatly interested Americans, the manufacture and sale being almost entirely given over to the English, Japanese, and Indian mills. Several sample shipments of the American product have been submitted to various importing houses of Tientsin and Niuchwang, but have not met with favorable reception on the part of the natives. Whether this is due more to the popularity of the "chops" of the mills now supplying these markets or to the lack of persistence in the efforts of our mills to obtain a foothold for their output here is not definitely ascertainable. Certain it is, however, that those who now find profit in selling this class of cottons are leaving nothing undone to retain their present hold upon the market and to stimulate the demand. T-cloths are among the cheaper cotton cloths and are well suited to the ability of the Japanese mills, which are rapidly increasing their sales in this market. From all information obtainable, therefore, the manufacture and sale of this style of unbleached cottons does not compete with the sale of any of the established American stuffs. Further than this, it has been ascertained from reliable native sources that the use of T-cloths is diminishing, their place being taken by cotton Italians to a great extent. Their use is, however, considerable among country people, who utilize them in making various articles of bedclothing, stockings, and garments.

WHITE GOODS.

Plain white shirtings and lawns constitute the bulk of the white goods sold in this market. White shirtings are used for making single suits for summer wear, stockings, and bed sheetings. When worn in white, it is a sign of mourning, and at other times the cloth is dyed in different shades of blue and gray. Not only is it used for single suits and garments, but it is also made into double garments for spring and fall wear. The prevailing widths are from 32 to 37 inches, although 36 inches may be said to be the maximum width, as it is seldom exceeded. Forty yards is the standard length, yet pieces run as high as 42 yards. White shirtings are not referred to by the weight per piece, as are gray shirtings and sheetings, but are valued by the quality, freedom from "size," finish, and general appearance. Those containing more sizing are cheaper in price and less serviceable for dyeing purposes. They are for the most part furnished by English mills, although in 1904 a portion of them came from America and a smaller quantity from the Netherlands.

While through Tientsin and Niuchwang 48.6 per cent of the gray cottons are sold and 78 per cent of these are from American mills, it is in the southern provinces that a greater field is offered for the expansion of new American enterprise—that is, for printed, dyed, and white goods—than is to be found in the north. The market in the north is, however, most attractive in that it consumed $4,100,635 of white, dyed, and printed goods, or nearly one-fourth of the Empire's importation of these cottons, in addition to presenting an almost limitless field for the increased sale of unbleached cottons, in the manufacture of which American mills have proven themselves superior to all others.

PRINTED AND DYED GOODS.

Among prints, which comprise a large proportion of this market's purchases, are all figured goods having a pattern printed on the cloth. These are styled "printed figured Italians," "printed figured cottons," and "metal prints." The great variety of print goods embraces single color and multicolor, printed turkey reds, T-cloths, lawns, muslins, cambrics, chintzes, furnitures, cretonnes, crapes, twills, crimp cloth, lenos, balzarines, sateens, reps, cotton lastings, and satinets. There is a diversity of finish, including gassed, mercerized, Schreiner, silk, electric finish, etc. This line offers a very attractive field for American exertion. There are many avenues through which success may be achieved, as there are many kinds and styles of prints in use.   Principal among these is printed T-cloth of 30-yard lengths or under, which constitute about 15 per cent of the imports. Printed T-cloth is made up into single coats for women and children for all seasons.   There is therefore a steady demand, the market extending inland to Turkestan, the most westerly province of China. All of the intervening territory is supplied with these goods, which follow the camel trade routes leading into the interior.

PRINTED REPS.

Printed reps and Italians are also in good demand. .These are used by the women of the better classes in the cities for making various articles of their ordinary or everyday clothing, while they serve the same purpose in making costumes for festival, anniversary, and special occasions for the better classes in the country.   The garments made from reps are for the most part worn in warm weather. The weaves do not exceed 32 inches in width and 32-yard lengths, ranging from 28 inches and 30 yards to the maximum widths and lengths.   These goods are delivered in Tientsin at prices ranging from about 12s. 6d. to 14s. 7d. for printed figured Italians, and from 9s. to 10s. for printed figured cottons.

CRIMP-CLOTH, FURNITURES, AND CRETONNES.

Printed crimp-cloth is a cheap cotton stuff, and finds favor in the country for making up single and double coats for women and girls. It is made in 30-inch widths and 30-yard lengths, and costs, laid down in north China ports, about 9s. to 9s. 11d. per piece.

Printed furnitures, printed crepes, reversible cretonnes, and figured lawns are being sold in increasing quantities.   The first three classes are used for making cushions and coverings for beds.   Printed figured lawns are used in making summer clothing for women and girls in the country and also to make mosquito curtains.   Furnitures are manufactured in 30-yard lengths and in widths varying from 30 to 36 inches, and are quoted at from 9s. to 12s. 9d.

Printed crepes are made in 29-inch widths and 25-yard lengths and are quoted at 4s. 8d. per piece.   The duty is based upon the same dimensions as printed T-cloths.   Among other prints may be mentioned printed lenos, which have a fair usage among the different provinces in making various garments for women and children.   They are woven in lengths not exceeding 30 yards, but more popularly in 12-yard lengths, and not exceeding 39 to 40 inches in width, with 36 to 37 inch widths having popular demand.

While there is a lucrative field for printed goods, yet dyed piece goods are more popular.   The total number of pieces of dyed cotton stuffs bought by Tientsin merchants for delivery during 1904 was 387,513, valued at $1,295,800, while in Niuchwang 119,535 pieces of dyed goods, at a valuation of $387,100, were imported during the same year. This represents a growing market and one worthy the careful attention of American cotton manufacturers.

ITALIANS.

Chief among the dyed cotton stuffs is the plain fast-black Italians. This cloth is much used in preference to drills and jeans. During the past four years its popularity has greatly increased by reason of its greater attractiveness in appearance and feeling and in its good lasting and wearing qualities. Its importation in 1904 exceeded $700,000 and comprised over 41 per cent of the dyed goods used in North China. Black cotton Italians having the greatest popularity are finished with a selvage of about one-fourth of an inch, in fine narrow stripes of alternating red and green. These selvages are usually woven of wool, and with the addition of these narrow borders such pieces bring from 1s. to 1s. 2d. more per piece. With the Chinese merchant and his patron these narrow bars are a stamp of quality higher than the same or better quality cloth without this kind of selvage. Borders having a simple alternating gray and black stripe will bring but from 1d. to 3d. advance over the plain black border.

Plain dyed colored Italians, mostly in purples and blues, are much worn by women, and like the black Italians are taking the place held by drills and jeans to a great extent. The prices of colored Italians are lower than the prices for similar finishes in blacks. They are worn by men and women of all classes in all seasons, though to a less extent in the summer. Figured or brocaded Italians in almost every color and shade are popular with residents of cities for making garments for both men and women, but their use is limited by the high price.

DYED TURKEY REDS AND COTTON FLANNELS.

Dyed Turkey red shirtings and cambrics are popular in the cities of Tientsin, Peking, and Niuchwang, and the surrounding provinces for making curtains for windows and clothing for girls and women. These cloths are woven in 30-inch widths and in 25 or 50 yard lengths to meet the general preferences, although certain requirements call for the usual 30-yard lengths. The prices per piece range from 6s. 4d. for 3½-pound stuff to 8s. 8d. for 6-pound stuff.

Cotton Spanish stripes are sold in large quantities. They are used principally in the Provinces of Pechili and Shansi. They are made into bedclothing and curtains, and it is customary to give them as presents at weddings, birthdays, and on other festive occasions. Merchants present their patrons with pieces of this kind of cloth on "opening days." In cotton flannels the American product leads English,

Japanese, and Dutch competitors. Cotton flannels come dyed in red, pink, heliotrope, plum, sky blue, scarlet, purple—in fact in every color, tint, and shade.

CLOTHING.

Chinese clothing may be divided into five classes or styles—single, double, wadded, fur, and gauze. Single garments—coats or other articles of clothing—are made of a single unlined piece of cloth. The "double" is single clothing with an inner lining, while "wadded" consists of three thicknesses, the outer cloth and inner lining having a layer of cotton batting between, generally quilted.

Single and gauze clothing is worn by men in summer, and consists of coat, trousers, and an outer flowing garment. In addition to these articles are shoes and stockings, the latter made of light-weight cloth and the shoes of cotton or satin. White cotton or satin is used for shoes if the wearer be in mourning. Another evidence of mourning is a length of white cord plaited into the queue, black being the color usually worn. In spring and autumn double coats, trousers, and leggins, with waistcoats, jackets, and double outer garments, are worn, and on cold days undergarments consisting of single coats or shirts and drawers are also worn. The clothing for mild winter weather consists of the same articles as those for fall and spring, with the exception that wadded coats and outer garments instead of double ones are used, while in severe weather fur waistcoats, jackets, and outer garments are worn in addition to all others, and boots take the place of shoes in most instances. Boots have wide tops, in which the flowing trousers are worn. The number of pieces of clothing worn by men is about the same in all classes. Five or six coats are usually worn one over the other in cold weather. The clothes of the higher classes differ from the other classes in that they are silk or other more expensive stuffs. The middle classes wear silk and cotton mixtures and finer cottons, and the lower classes cotton.

The dress of women and girls is similar to the clothing of men, although in treaty ports instances are found of the adoption by women of many articles of dress worn by foreign women. In addition to men's clothing named above, head coverings and temple bands, petticoats, and foot bands are worn by women. The shoes worn by women differ greatly in shape from men's shoes, but the material of which they are made is similar.

Bedclothing, while not generally classed as ordinary clothing, is considered among the essentials of a complete wardrobe, in that no Chinese person is admitted to the native inns unless possessed of bedclothing. A set of bedclothing consists of an underpiece and a coverlet, both generally wadded with cotton batting. The upper surface is made of figured cotton or silk, while the lining is of sheeting or shirting.

Sheetings, especially those from America, and native woven cloth dyed in various shades of blue are much used by the country people for all kinds of clothing. The cost of dyeing varies somewhat according to conditions, but approximates $1.50 gold per piece.

COTTON SPECIALTIES.

Cotton blankets of German and English manufacture are sold in this market in good quantities. The lighter weights are scarcely heavier than outing flannel of good weight, while the heavier ones are slightly better. These blankets have an ever increasing field of distribution, not only in the immediate market afforded by the Province of Pechili, but also in the Provinces of Honan, Shansi, and Shensi. Many of them find their way into the interior as far as Kansuh Province and into the northern Manchurian market, the province of Kirin being a large buyer. Blankets most desired are those of bright scarlet.

TOWELS AND HANDKERCHIEFS.

Towels are used throughout all the territory to which Tientsin and Niuchwang are the gateways. Japanese mills at present control the market. The towels are of light weight and flimsy for the most part, although a considerable quantity of the better qualities are purchased by the wealthier classes. In size towels vary from 12 to 18 inches in the most popular widths and in lengths from 30 to 40 and even as long as 50 inches. The greatest number in use are those having printed or stamped designs of oriental types in blue and black, the most popular colors.

There is a large and increasing use of cheap cotton handkerchiefs, made especially for this market by Japanese manufacturers. These have oriental designs, figures, and characters of peculiar significance to the purchasers. Germany and England also send a large quantity of cheap handkerchiefs, which find a ready market. The goods from which they are made is exceedingly cheap, and they sell at from 24.5 cents to 63 cents gold per dozen. Higher prices are obtained for better qualities.

THREAD, LACE, AND BRAIDS.

Cotton thread on spools and in balls is used extensively. All sizes or counts of cotton spool thread, both glazed and unglazed, are used, but by far the greatest use is made of Nos. 8, 10, 50, and 60 six-cord, in 200-yard lengths; these retail at 8 cents Mexican (4 cents United States currency). The spool is differently shaped from that in ordinary use in America.

Cotton lace figures quite largely in the articles coming into Tientsin for native uses. The sizes most in use are 2-inch and 2½-inch, and are quoted c. i. f. Tientsin at £16 in cases of 1,000 cards, each containing

6 yards of lace. These cases are packed for shipment with two-thirds of the lace in 2-inch widths, while the remaining one-third is made up of 2½-inch widths.

Cotton or Llama braid is much in use by the Chinese in trimming different garments. It comes from England and France in large quantities, in widths varying from one-eighth of an inch to one-half inch and in all colors and shades. The blacks are the cheapest, being less in price per 144 yards. Braid of this character is laid down in Tientsin in three grades, each piece containing 144 yards: Cheapest grade, 1s. 11d. to 2s. 1d.; medium grade, 2s. 1½d. to 5s. 7½d.; best grade, 2s. 7d. to 6s. 8d.

Imitation gold and silver thread finds a good market in Pechili and is distributed throughout the northern and western provinces in varying amounts. This product comes almost entirely from Germany, and a current price f. o. b. Hamburg for best gold thread, per 133⅓ pounds, is $60.27; best quality silver thread, $70.11. Cheaper grades of gold thread are laid down at $55.35, and the same grade of silver thread at $45.01 per picul. Gold and silver thread are done up in rolls containing 50 hanks of 1 yard each, wrapped in tissue paper and a paper cover carrying trade-mark. They are shipped in tin-lined wooden cases.

YARNS.

Yarn forms one of the most important branches of the cotton trade. It is purchased by the natives of north China in greater quantities than ever before. Its use extends throughout the Empire and has been especially in evidence during those periods when the price of cotton has caused such advances in the cost of piece goods as to curtail their purchase. At such times the natives obtain from the hand loom the substitute for the cloth which under ordinary conditions would be imported from abroad. This is not the only influence actuating the purchase of foreign as well as native spun yarns, for the adherence to old established customs and habits is also potent and will be felt for years to come.

FOREIGN YARN FOR NATIVE LOOMS.

The native population of the hinterland, in which the foreign-made commodities are distributed from these ports, is only partially acquainted with the imported cotton products, and in many sections the people still rely upon the slow process of hand weaving from native cotton. In other localities, on account of the prohibitive cost of the foreign-made textile, great quantities of imported cotton yarns go to form the warp and weft of the product of the hand looms. The wool of the camel, sheep, and goat and the furs and skins of various animals, both domestic and wild, also contribute toward the supply of stuffs from which the native garments are fashioned.

The purchase of foreign cotton yarns by the ports of Tientsin and Niuchwang more than doubled in the ten years ending 1903, when these two ports received 33,310,133 pounds out of a total importation by the Empire of 365,000,000 pounds. This is no unusual purchase, as it has been exceeded in other years, notably 1898, 1899, 1902, and 1904, when it exceeded 40,500,000 pounds, and in all likelihood 1900 and 1901 would have equaled 1903 but for the disturbance of the Boxer uprising.

This immense business is in the hands of Indian, Japanese, and English yarn spinners, American mills being practically without representation. A good market can be found in China for the products of a great number of spinning mills, and their establishment would appear to be justified by the immense field which China alone presents. A prominent American authority has stated that an average price of 27½ cents per pound was maintained in 1904 by English mills in the sale of over 160,000,000 pounds of cotton yarns in foreign countries.

There is nothing peculiar to the export and sale of cotton yarns, unless it be that the bales require better and more careful treatment than is given to raw cotton. If cotton yarn were baled with the same kind of covering that is used for raw cotton, every shipment would be ruined. Inasmuch as this is a new field for American enterprise, it would be well to adopt that style of packing which represents the experience of those countries that have successfully engaged in the export of yarns for many years.

Yarns are packed in bales, machine pressed, containing 40 packages, each package weighing 10 pounds, and having 20 skeins. Each package is inclosed in medium-weight wrapping paper and the whole covered with heavy wrapping paper. This is, in turn, wrapped with heavy tarred gunny sacking, and over all there is placed a close-woven gunny-sack covering. From four to six heavy iron straps bind the bale, the edges of which are supported by strong wooden strips laid lengthwise on the sides of the bale. This is the method pursued by English, Indian, and Japanese importers, with the exception that the Japanese do not use the tarred gunny cloth, as the liability to damage by moisture does not figure so greatly in the comparatively short passage from Osaka or other Japanese ports to the Chinese market.

One particular point is in strong evidence in the Japanese yarns, and that is in the matter of weight. All cotton yarns are imported at prices calculated to the bale, which ordinarily is 400 pounds net. English and Indian yarns are shipped in bales of 400 pounds net weight of cotton, while Japanese yarn has a net weight of 420 pounds per bale, or 5 per cent more yarn per bale than English or Indian yarns, although invoiced at 400 pounds net. At first glance this may appear to lend an exceedingly attractive appearance to Japanese yarns; but when it is known that this added weight is produced by moisture, which ultimately has a deteriorating effect upon the yarn, it becomes apparent that in the hands of shrewd Chinese buyers a comparison with the "A first" grade American yarn would lead to a decision in favor of the latter.   It can be safely stated that not one Chinese in a thousand among the great number of users of American sheetings knows anything of the source from which they come.   The only thing he knows about them is that for years he has bought these cloths with this or that kind of chop (trade-mark) printed on them, and they have made good, lasting clothing for him, and he will take no other.   And so it would be with our yarns if their sale in this territory were undertaken.

IV. MISCELLANEOUS IMPORTS.

VARIOUS ARTICLES WORTH CONSIDERING.

PIECE GOODS.

The woolen piece goods imported for native use are principally blankets and rugs; English camlets; habit, medium, and broad cloth; plain figured and creped lastings; long ells, and Spanish stripes. The most important of these are the woolen lastings, for which there is an annual market worth about $40,000, and English camlets of which about $30,000 worth are sold. The former measure 31 inches in width and average 30 yards in length. They enter quite extensively into the material of which jackets, shoes, and trimmings for clothing are made. English camlets are used largely in the uniforms of the army and for other military purposes, and for this reason there should be a large market for their sale in the near future. The other kinds of woolen goods on this market are sold in small quantities.

Cotton and woolen mixtures constitute a small item in the foreign trade of north China. Among miscellaneous piece goods, silk piece goods and velvets, plushes, and silk seal with cotton back are the most important.

FOOTWEAR.

The shoes worn by Chinese are pronounced in their difference from the American article and are cheaply made, the cost of production compared with their selling price being quite low. A fair estimate of the value of the cloth and leather entering into the construction of the average Chinese shoe places the amount at about 10 cents. The principal item of expense is the leather strip forming the sole, which extends the full length of the shoe, there being no raised heel. Shoes and boots with velvet vamps and tops have about 20 cents' worth of material in their construction. An examination in detail of the parts of shoes before assembling discloses the flimsiness of their make. Scraps of paper and blue or black sheeting or shirting pasted together constitute the uppers. There are various styles in use in north China, both high and low quarter. Low-quarter shoes made of dyed cotton or black satin are worn at all seasons by the masses, and their prices range from 50 to 75 cents per pair. High shoes or boots are worn by the soldiers and police as well as by the merchants and all classes except the poorest, the prices ranging from

75 cents for the unlined cloth boots to $1.25 for fleece-lined velvet boots. Leather boots for army and police purposes cost $1.75 and are in great demand at present in view of the increase of the Chinese army. The average life of a pair of Chinese shoes is one month.

RIBBONS.

One of the large items of import is ribbons. Both silk and silk-mixture ribbons are bought in large quantities and are distributed through the various Chinese channels to the farthest corners of the Empire. In the making of almost every article of wearing apparel of the Chinese woman a large use is made of ribbons, both for utility and decoration. The vestments of Chinese mandarins furnish opportunities for employing untold quantities of embroideries and ribbons, many colored and figured. Ribbons are also used to a great extent by the better classes as ankle straps with which to bind the extremities of their flowing trousers. These ribbons are almost all of French and native manufacture.

Five-color ribbons appear to be the most popular styles, and upon this basis orders will be filled in any design in lots of 240 pieces of 18 yards per piece, while lots as small as 10 pieces of 18-yard lengths will be specially woven in the designs represented by the samples sent out by the manufacturers in any colors the Chinese may elect, all limited to five colors—that is, four colors and the ground color.

BUTTONS.

The importation of brass and fancy buttons is a very important and valuable branch of the foreign trade of Tientsin. The bulk of these comes from Germany. Buttons having the appearance of either brass or silver are more popular than the fancy buttons. The latter are made in various styles, the ornamental parts being of varicolored glass in oriental or other designs, with a brass or silver foundation. The most popular of the brass buttons come in "globe" or ball pattern, and in three sizes, 4½, 5, or 5½ lines, with ground surfaces worked up in a great variety of fancy decorations. Upon this ground there is stamped, upon the selection of the Chinese merchant, a suitable design, consisting generally of some conventional figure or Chinese character signifying happiness, wealth, or long life, or the figure of some creature occupying a prominent place in Chinese life or faith.

It is the practice among button manufacturers to forward a great variety of samples, practically covering their entire output. These styles necessarily embrace many that are entirely unsuited to the demands of this market. The great variety, however, affords the Chinese an opportunity to select some new style which may appeal to his ancy, and in this manner new kinds are being taken up continually, with a consequent broadening of the field of sale as well as correspondingly increasing the hold of the manufacturer's goods upon the market.

The globe buttons are sent incomplete that selection may be made of the style of groundwork, upon which the manufacturer will stamp any design suited to the taste of the Chinese patron. These are sent out in all of the preferred sizes in brass and white metal, or, as they are technically referred to in the trade, "gold and silver." Tentative designs are also submitted for inspection and selection.

All buttons used here have rings in addition to shanks, in order to admit of changing from one garment to another and of removal during washing. Buttons without rings will have no sale. Each silver button requires a silver shank and a silver ring, while brass buttons require brass shanks and rings.

SOAP.

The item of bar soap is of considerable importance in this part of China, amounting in 1904 to 18,951 piculs of 133⅓ pounds, at a customs valuation of $93,310 gold. Most of this soap is of English make. The qualities desired are dryness and hardness, without much shrinking or loss of weight upon being kept for a length of time. It is made in 13-inch lengths, 2 by 1½ inches, the bar weighing approximately 2 pounds. The retail prices prevailing are about $2.85 per box of 24 bars and from 12½ to 15 cents per bar. Shipments are made in boxes containing 24 bars. There have been expressions from various importers here favorable to the introduction of American soaps, all stating the belief that it can be done successfully if properly undertaken.

The increasing use of toilet soaps of varying prices and grades does not seem to attract American manufacturers as much as it does the Japanese, English, Dutch, French, Austrian, and German. In the year 1904 the valuation placed on these imports was $75,544. Most of this was used within the immediate neighborhood of the ports, but nearly $26,000 worth was distributed throughout the vast territory supplied by Tientsin, finding its way as far westward as Chinese Turkestan. The principal claim of European soaps upon popularity rests upon the fact that they are pushed by their several makers. Commercial travelers with various lines of soap are sent out twice a year to acquaint themselves with the latest tendencies of the market. That American manufacturers might build up a valuable clientele in the Orient by the same methods or by establishing agencies with importers for the sale of their product there is slight reason to doubt.

The popular toilet soaps are of the cheaper kinds, highly scented in the different odors of rose, heliotrope, violet, and almost all of the scents in use in the American market. There is also a growing demand for the higher qualities with delicate scenting in the odors above referred to. The prices are similar to those prevailing at home.

CANDLES.

Tientsin and Niuchwang received during 1904 1,097,133 pounds of candles, valued at $99,953, two-thirds going to Niuchwang. Most of these were manufactured in England and in great part in one factory. They come in boxes containing 25 packages of 6 candles each, with a covering of light paraffin paper, the whole wrapped in blue unglazed wrapping paper, with the ends sealed by wax wafers. Upon the wrapper is pasted the label giving the brand. White candles are used for ordinary illuminating purposes, while colored candles—scarlet most popular—are used on festal occasions, holidays, weddings, and birthdays. Nine-ounce white candles retail at 8 cents per package of six, 12-ounce at 9 cents, and 15-ounce at 10 cents; colored candles bring higher prices in the same weights, viz, 10 cents, 15 cents, and $17\frac{1}{2}$ cents, respectively.

LOOKING-GLASSES.

Looking-glasses and mirrors of small size are being sold in great quantities by the Japanese makers. Glasses of all sizes from the small hand mirror about the size of an American silver dollar up to full-length cheval mirrors are made by the Japanese for this market. A popular variety is mounted upon a metal stand made of heavy wire, nickel plated, so as to swing upon pivots. These are almost entirely of Japanese make, and in sizes ranging from 6 by 3 up to 8 by 12 or 9 by 12 inches, with beveled edges and rounded corners or oval shapes. They are laid down here, including freight and insurance, at from 70 cents to $1.25 each United States currency. Beveled-edge glass mirrors mounted on wooden backs with adjustable wire brace at back, 4 by 6 inches, sell at 45 cents Mexican each and $4 Mexican per dozen. Larger sizes, 8 by 6 inches, sell at 85 cents each and $8 per dozen Mexican (about $42\frac{1}{2}$ cents and $4, respectively, American).

METALS AND MANUFACTURES.

IRON, COPPER, AND LEAD.

One of the principal imports of metals is old iron, which comes in great quantities from Holland, Germany, and other European countries and enters largely into the domestic economy in the production of many of the various articles of daily necessity. Among these are razors, knives, hammers, hatchets and other chopping implements, plowshares, shovels, various tools for the different trades, metal for stove castings, and other cast-iron products. Through Tientsin and

Niuchwang upward of $360,000 worth of old iron is annually imported, three-fourths of this going through Niuchwang. This old iron consists of horseshoes, old plate and sheet iron, railway spikes, cart tires, hoop and scrap iron. Old horseshoes constitute the principal of these, often exceeding $100,000 in value.

Iron and steel bars and angles, bolts, nuts, washers, wire nails, steel wire, pipe, and tubing constitute the most important of the other steel and iron imports. Galvanized iron in corrugated and plain sheets and galvanized-iron wire offer a market of upward of $120,000, divided about equally between the ports of Niuchwang and Tientsin. In these lines the English manufacturers predominate, comparatively little, if any, of the American product being in evidence.

Other metals, such as copper, nickel, lead in pipes, pigs, bars, tea-lead, and tin sheets and slabs, constitute the remainder of a market of $1,389,000 for various metals.

ENAMELED WARE.

Sales of enameled-ware utensils are steadily increasing throughout this part of the Empire. Seventy per cent of these importations find purchasers in the Province of Pechili. The Austrian manufacturers control the market.

Very little of the American product up to the present finds its way into this market, but that it can be introduced in competition with the European article there is little doubt. Decorated enameled ware is limited in sale to the cities, where the Chinese have a greater purchasing power, while the plain ware has a large sale in all towns and cities, and throughout the provinces. The articles most in use are ordinary plain wash basins, blue outside and white inside, having a rim diameter of from 9 to 15 inches. Basins decorated on the white inside ground with gaudily colored flowers or figures of occidental design also take well. I mention particularly occidental and not oriental designs, for in this particular line of goods the Chinese appear to prefer the artistic creations of the Western mind. Three or four designs are placed on the inner side of wash basins, with one bottom figure, also on the inner side, and the decoration may be either raised or smooth. Enameled wash basins are quoted at prices varying according to their dimensions and color of enameling—whether light or dark blue or pink. Blue enameled teakettles of different capacities, ranging from 1 to 3 quarts, are good sellers.

NEEDLES.

The greatest portion of this market's purchases of needles is doubtless controlled by the German production, and the method pursued by Germans in packing is the most desirable to be followed by American houses in shipping needles to the oriental market. German needles are packed in small packages containing 25 needles, wrapped in black paper, with the usual opening for removing the needles, and having a label pasted upon the side indicating the number of the needles. These small packages are tied in bundles of ten each and then wrapped in black paper, around which is generally placed a light-weight manila-paper wrapper tied with white cord. This is in turn wrapped in a second manila-paper wrapping and securely tied with strong, light-weight twine, and the whole placed in a tin case, which is soldered, thereby making it moisture proof. Upon this case the labels are placed, both in English and in Chinese characters, one on each side. A wrapping of heavy brown paper incloses this, securely tied with stout cord. One hundred cases of this kind, all cases containing the same kinds of needles, are packed in a zinc-lined wooden box for shipment. The zinc lining is carefully soldered to make it moisture and water proof.

The annual purchase of needles is steadily increasing, and there is a demand for cheap needles of sizes ranging from 1, 1½, and 2 inches to as great lengths as are usual in ordinary darning needles. In the last calendar year there were sold in this market, of almost wholly German and English manufacture, 350,102 mille, at a valuation of 105,030 haikwan taels (almost $70,000). These needles are all coarse, and have large eyes, to be of use to the poorer classes in sewing with the coarser counts of thread, which are most in use by the natives.

CLOCKS.

Nickel-plated alarm clocks of German make sell for an equivalent of 80 cents United States currency, while nickel-plated brass-trimmed clocks, oblong shaped, about 6½ or 7 inches in height, with alarms, sell at prices equaling $1.50 gold. The same sized clock with music-box attachment, playing Chinese music, sells at $2 gold values. American seven-day clocks are most popular among the better classes of Chinese and sell at local currency values equaling $6 United States gold. There is, however, a greater demand for cheaper clocks, similar in appearance, which is being supplied in great part by Japanese makers. These sell at prices from $2.25 to $3 gold each. The Chinese recognize the superior quality of American clocks and watches over the Japanese and German makes. The matter of price, however, has a large influence in transactions, and purchasers often take the cheap article instead of the one of better quality simply because of the lower cost, although they are quick to place the proper values upon the genuine article and the spurious imitation.

V. ARTICLES OF EXPORT.

The stimulus which will be given to the purchase of imports by the development of China's resources will also be felt in the matter of exports. No country can continue in the market as a buyer nation only, but must also have recourse to its ability to sell its products in order as nearly as possible to keep the proper balance between the two sides of the ledger. Although the exports from Tientsin represent only about one-third, and sometimes not so much, of the value of the imports from foreign countries, the export business is commanding constantly growing attention from local business houses. With Niuchwang, however, the disparity between exports and imports is not so marked. Fully 50 per cent of the commodities comprising this branch of the foreign trade of Tientsin are destined for America, although the Chinese customs returns for 1904 show $8,465,171 out of a total of $9,830,970 as destined for Chinese ports. This arises from the fact that direct shipment is made to Shanghai, where transshipments are effected to vessels bound for foreign countries. The bulk of the Niuchwang exports is made up of beans, bean-cake and bean oil, and wild raw silk, the former aggregating $5,000,000 and the latter nearly a million dollars in favorable years, and is practically all destined for Japan.

The principal commodities making up the export trade of Tientsin are sheep's wool, skins of goat, sheep, and lamb, coal, straw braid, bristles, goat and sheep rugs, and groundnuts. All of the above-named articles of export are for foreign consumption with the exception of coal and groundnuts. Sheep's wool stands first on the list, with $2,005,560; skins, $1,105,828; bristles, $705,568; rugs, $696,672; straw braid, $631,934; groundnuts, $448,622, and coal, $125,000.

WOOL.

The exportation of sheep's wool from Tientsin has been growing constantly during the past twenty years, although there have been periods of unusual increases, due in great part to changes or proposed changes in the tariff law of the United States. In 1893, when there was a possibility of a reduction of the tariff, a congestion of wools resulted in anticipation of this action, while in 1899 the reverse was the order. Since 1901 the standard of wools exported has on the whole been considerably higher, as a large percentage has been machine cleaned. In the decade 1889–1899 the average annual shipment was 76,907 piculs (133⅓ pounds each) of uncleaned wool, and from 1895 to 1904 the average rose to 149,998 piculs of a better cleaned and more valuable wool. That this increase had taken place during the decade in which the Boxer uprising occurred speaks well for the possibilities of this trade, especially when a quicker and cheaper mode of transportation is afforded by the construction of railways. With the completion of the Peking-Kalgan Railroad into the border of the great wool-growing district of Mongolia there will be a resulting increase in the export of wool.

RAILROADS WOULD INCREASE EXPORTS.

Not only would the development of railroads be of material benefit to the wool trade, but it would be a boon to all other exports. The greatly increased exportation of straw braid from Pechili and Honan by way of Kiao Chow has proved that the railroad, the surest and easiest method of transportation, will readily supersede the antiquated camel and water routes. While Tibet furnishes the finest grade of lambskins, the region around Kalgan supplies the second and third grades, known as "fine and rough Kalgans," and Mongolia the fourth grade. What is true of the effect of a railroad to Kalgan upon Mongolian products applies with greater force to the farther distant interior. From Tibet only the most valuable skins and other products of small bulk can now be brought down at a profit, whereas with modern transportation much coarser produce could come out to exchange for additional foreign commodities. The choice sheep and goat skins are obtained in Shansi Province, while the second quality comes from southwestern Pechili. Bristles come from the wide area embraced by Manchuria, Pechili, and Shantung.

EFFECT OF ADULTERATION OF PRODUCTS.

Ten years ago straw braid was the leading native product exported from Tientsin, but it has declined in volume and in relative importance by reason of the adulteration and tampering which have been indulged in by its producers. In fact, this is the universal complaint in regard to the leading native produce—tea, silk, bristles, feathers, horsehair, etc. The export of straw plait from Tientsin has been greatly reduced by the evidences of poor workmanship and bad quality of the straw. It is no uncommon experience, I am informed by one of the former leading exporters of this commodity, to find in one bundle of plait strands 4½ and 6 millimeters and in another 7 and 8 millimeters and 9 and 10 millimeters side by side. This, coupled with the red and green straws that no amount of bleaching can make white, tells the story. If these irregularities and imperfections should be overcome, there is belief among those qualified to speak on the subject that there would be a revival in this trade. At present, according to the last Kiao Chow Trade Report, it would appear that much of this trade is going south by rail to that port. Among the adulterants used in other of the native produce are short lengths and soft hairs in bristles; false packing and watering in all grades of horsehair; dirt in feathers to increase their weight; giving shorter measure pieces in skins and in patching with inferior pieces to the bulk; in lambskins, water, flour, and chopsticks are the originators of many of the supposedly genuine curls. Untanned skins are badly dressed and many are rendered valueless by bad knife work. In camel's, goat's, and sheep's wool the chief feature of adulteration consists of sand and dirt of all descriptions, while as for such fancy furs as sables and ermine prices are greatly advanced beyond values, and no one but an expert is able to buy without risk of being imposed upon by the many specious forms under which they are offered.

PACKING FOR TRANSPORTATION.

In connection with the work of counteracting this tendency of the producers to make their wares unfit for market use, it is interesting to delve a bit into the processes of cleaning the wools and skins and packing them for shipment. Such cargoes as will permit are put into hydraulic presses and submitted to a very heavy pressure in order to effect an economy in space and consequently in freight and handling charges. The first plant to do public packing was erected about fifteen years ago, and now there are four firms that make a business of it. This method of treating outgoing cargo was naturally evolved to meet the high freight rates over long runs and has accomplished an economy which alone makes it possible in certain commodities to withstand the growing competition of other sources of supply.

The principal cargoes subjected to this process are sheep's, goat's, and camel's wool, cotton, jute, untanned goat and sheep skins, goat rugs, and cowhides. The packing is performed by heavy hydraulic presses, to which power is supplied by multiplex pumps directly connected to steam engines. The most powerful of the presses are devoted to loose cargo, such as wool, jute, and cotton, and can develop a total compressive force between the heads approximating 1,000 long tons. Thus the lower ram in this type exerts power enough to lift bodily a steamer of the class devoted to the Tientsin-Shanghai trade. It compresses wool to a density of water. The skin and rug presses are less powerful only because this class of cargo may not be subjected to the same treatment without danger of ruin. The variation of maximum and minimum densities is due to a number of coexistent causes, such as the presence of dirt and grease in wools, which conduce to greater density, and of moisture, which increases the density to a remarkable degree. On the other hand, the resilience of dry and clean wools is such as to cause enormous stresses on the baling hoop, which, although of the very best ductile steel, has been observed under such stress to elongate as much as 10 per cent.

To show the actual results accomplished, one need but state that wool arrives at the cleaning loft in native bags, with a capacity of 20 cubic feet and a weight of about 1 picul (133⅓ pounds), and leaves the presses in bales measuring 10 cubic feet and weighing 650 pounds. In other words, the package is reduced by the process to one-tenth of its original bulk. This ratio of compression, 10 units into 1, may be taken as about the average. And when it is remembered that freight charges are largely made on the basis of displacement, and that very often handling fees are assessed per bale, it will at once be seen what an important part this press packing has come to play in the export business.

The cost of packing, together with that of the cleaning to which the cargo is subjected before being put in the presses, amounts on the average to about 6 per cent of the value

INDEX.

O

For Product Safety Concerns and Information please contact our EU representative GPSR@taylorandfrancis.com Taylor & Francis Verlag GmbH, Kaufingerstraße 24, 80331 München, Germany

Printed and bound by CPI Group (UK) Ltd, Croydon, CR0 4YY

12/05/2025

01867562-0001